Series / Number 07-015

# MULTIPLE INDICATORS
## An Introduction

**JOHN L. SULLIVAN**
*University of Minnesota*

**STANLEY FELDMAN**
*Brown University*

SAGE PUBLICATIONS / Beverly Hills / London

*For information address:*

SAGE Publications, Inc.   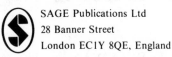   SAGE Publications Ltd
275 South Beverly Drive        28 Banner Street
Beverly Hills, California 90212        London EC1Y 8QE, England

International Standard Book Number 0-8039-1369-9

Library of Congress Catalog Card No. L.C. 79-67015

FIRST PRINTING

When citing a professional paper, please use the proper form. Remember to cite the correct
Sage University Paper series title and include the paper number. One of the two following
formats can be adapted (depending on the style manual used):

(1) IVERSEN, GUDMUND R. and NORPOTH, HELMUT (1976) "Analysis of Variance." Sage University Paper series on Quantitative Applications in the Social Sciences,
07-001. Beverly Hills and London: Sage Pubns.

*OR*

(2) Iversen, Gudmund R. and Norpoth, Helmut. 1976. *Analysis of Variance.* Sage University Paper series on Quantitative Applications in the Social Sciences, series no. 07-001.
Beverly Hills and London: Sage Publications.

# CONTENTS

Editor's Introduction   5

Preface   8

Introduction   9

**Validity, Reliability, and Multiple Indicators   16**
   Campbell and Fiske's Multitrait-Multimethod Matrix   17
   An Application of the Multitrait-Multimethod Matrix to
      Achievement Motivation   25
   Costner's Multiple-Indicator Approach to
      Reliability Assessment   28
   Extensions to More Concepts   35
   Extensions to More Indicators   38
   An Example Applying Costner's Procedures   40

**Critique of Multitrait-Multimethod Matrix   47**

**Multiple-Indicator Models for Panel Data   56**
   Applications to Panel Data of Party Identification and
      Attitudes Toward Political Parties   66

**Conclusions   70**
   Hypothesis Testing   70
   Estimation   73
   Multiple-Indicator Models: Some Final Considerations   75

**Appendix A: Some Basic Statistical Concepts   76**
   Populations and Samples   76
   Parameters and Estimates   76
   Bias and Efficiency   77
   Identification   77

**Appendix B: The Wiley and Wiley Three-Wave,
  One-Indicator Model   79**

Notes   82

References   84

**Editor's Introduction**

MULTIPLE INDICATORS: AN INTRODUCTION by John L. Sullivan and Stanley Feldman complements well one of the earlier papers in the series, CAUSAL MODELING by Herbert B. Asher. The reader should either be knowledgeable about causal modeling techniques or should study the Asher volume carefully before attempting to read this paper. In addition, it would be helpful if the reader also has an elementary knowledge of regression analysis and measurement theory before undertaking this paper.

Multiple-indicator techniques are useful for both individual and aggregate data analysis applications which involve either cross-sectional or longitudinal research designs. Based upon the general linear model, the techniques provide a rigorous way to link theory and data in the social sciences. Using these techniques, a researcher can specify a model of theoretical relationships with empirical indicators of the concepts embodied in the model. The techniques Sullivan and Feldman outline provide methods by which a researcher may choose among alternative indicators for concepts as the researcher proceeds to specify a theoretical model. In essence, these techniques make it possible for researchers to specify theoretical models more systematically.

Sullivan and Feldman introduce several techniques in this paper which permit the researcher to assess the validity and reliability of empirical indicators used to measure concepts in simple theoretical models. The emphasis is on elementary techniques to assess the validity and reliability of measures, and the authors have simplified the conceptual models presented to illustrate the utility of the techniques. Throughout the paper the mathematics are kept at an introductory level. A reader with a working knowledge of elementary algebra should experience no difficulty in following the mathematical presentations.

In their discussion of validity and reliability assessment, Sullivan and Feldman present two different approaches for dealing with these measurement problems. First, they detail the multitrait-multimethod matrix technique and show how it is used to choose among alternative indicators of a concept and alternative methods for measuring those indicators. They employ an example involving the measurement of achievement motivation to illustrate the utility of the technique. Second, they outline a multiple-indicator approach to reliability assessment devised by Costner and demonstrate the value of the technique for analysis applications involving aggregate data. Using an example from the literature of American state politics, they lucidly show how to select among alternative indicators when the data do not meet the conditions needed by the multiple-indicator approach to measurement error assessment. In the process of discussing the two approaches to the assessment of measurement error, they do the reader a service by using one clear-cut example involving individual level data while making the other example an illustration of a technique appropriate for aggregate data. No matter what type of previous experience the reader has had with data analysis, one or both of the examples are certain to seem familiar.

Following a critique of the multitrait-multimethod matrix approach, the authors outline how multiple-indicator methods can be employed with data stemming from panel designs. Even though the models become consistently more complex in this section of the paper, the authors nicely take the reader step by step through applications involving simple two-wave, one-indicator models all the way through relatively sophisticated multi-wave, multiple-indicator models. In this progression from the simple to the complex, Sullivan and Feldman are very careful to ensure that each new model builds upon the previous one and that nothing is left to the imagination of the reader. Examples are then presented using panel survey data to assess the reliability and stability of repeated measures of party identification in the United States and of political party evaluations in Great Britain. These examples clearly demonstrate how valuable the multiple-indicator approach can be for the assessment of measurement error in panel data.

The paper concludes, then, with introductory discussions of hypothesis testing with multiple-indicator models, parameter estimation based on those models, and the general problems associated with multiple-indicator techniques. Although the authors are advocating that other researchers adopt the multiple-indicator approach for assessing measurement error, continually throughout the paper they discuss forthrightly the limitations as well as the advantages of the technique. For the reader who is unfamiliar with some of the basic terms used in this paper, the authors have included an appendix in which they discuss the basic statistical concepts underlying the multiple-indicator approach.

The multiple-indicator approach that Sullivan and Feldman outlined can be appropriately used in a number of social science disciplines; the examples in the paper demonstrate uses in sociology and political science. In addition, the psychologist or educator might find applications for these techniques in both experimental and nonexperimental research. The economist might employ them fruitfully in modeling either microeconomic or macroeconomic behavior. Quantitative historians might find these techniques appropriate in attempting to choose among possible indicators of historical change. All in all, many social scientists can learn much about measurement error in their data by employing the techniques presented in MULTIPLE INDICATORS: AN INTRODUCTION

—Ronald E. Weber, Editorial Board

## PREFACE

In this short monograph, we hope to introduce the reader to some simple techniques which allow one to address the problem of validity and reliability of measurement procedures and the resultant measures. Since the techniques are simple, they are most useful when applied to simple hypotheses and theories, as represented by simple models. These techniques, the multitrait multimethod approach and the multiple-indicator approach, both involve th the use of multiple measures, or indicators, of abstract concepts or traits. And although they are simple to understand and to use, they are nevertheless powerful aids for assessing the validity and reliability of measures.

It is our ultimate purpose, however, to convince the reader that for more complex problems and more complicated models, the usefulness of these simple procedures is greatly limited. We plan, in a companion paper (forthcoming), to present more complicated alternatives which can be used appropriately and powerfully with models which become increasingly realistic and complex, i.e., models which involve large numbers of variables measured with multiple indicators. So we hope to whet the readers' appetites by demonstrating the power of simple techniques, trusting that this will cause our readers to explore the more complicated procedures of maximum likelihood estimation techniques and the analysis of covariance structures, which are infinitely more powerful than the procedures discussed herein.

We wish to acknowledge the valuable criticism on an earlier version of this monograph provided by Mr. William Berry and by the anonymous referees for this series. We also own an intellectual debt to Professor Hubert M. Blalock, Jr.

# INTRODUCTION

Social scientists involved in empirical research frequently work simultaneously in two related but analytically distinct spheres. On the one hand, they develop theoretical explanations for the phenomena under study. These need not be highly developed theories, but may be simple hypotheses formulated as a means of guiding the research. One common aspect of these hypotheses, whether developed in isolation or as elements of an elaborate theory, is that they specify relationships between abstract *concepts* or *constructs*. It is this characteristic that most clearly distinguishes the theoretical level of analysis. So, for example, a political scientist might be interested in the political impact of urbanization on political development or the relationship between ideology and political cynicism, while a sociologist might be concerned with the effects of social status on occupational aspirations. In each case, the concept would first be given a *conceptual definition* that would establish its meaning in terms of other theoretical and abstract terms.

While the development of theories and hypotheses might satisfy the needs of a political or social theorist, the researcher must also be concerned with a second level of analysis. Here the primary emphasis is on testing the abstract hypotheses using empirical data. In order to empirically test a hypothesis employing abstract concepts, we must specify observable and measurable characteristics of the units or cases under study (e.g., people, states, nations, and such) that reflect the nature of the abstract concepts included. These measurable, empirically grounded characteristics are referred to as *indicators* of the concepts. With respect to the examples previously cited, the political scientist might measure ideology by asking people a series of questions on public policy issues, presenting both liberal and conservative alternatives. The number of liberal responses given could then be summed to produce the desired indicator. Similarly, the sociologist could assess the subjects' number of years of education to obtain a measure of social status. It is not difficult to think of alternative indicators for each of these concepts.

The distinction being made here is critical for understanding many of the fundamental problems in conducting research in the social sciences. Emerging from this is what Blalock (1968) has termed "the measurement problem," a gap between theoretical concepts and empirical indicators of those concepts. At the heart of the matter is the crucial realization that we cannot *directly* test hypotheses based upon abstract concepts. In fact, if scope and generality are criteria by which an explanation is to be judged, any concept which may be directly measured would indicate a poorly formulated theory or hypothesis. If, for example, our political scientist concerned with ideology initially *defined* the concept in terms of the measure of issue positions, the results of the research would at best provide a description of current patterns of political attitudes. It could not, however, provide a *general* explanation of the relationship between ideology and cynicism since the meaning of ideology would change or become obsolete as the nature of the political issues changes. Thus, it is only by defining terms first at an abstract or conceptual level that researchers can achieve the desired significance for their explanations.

Since abstract concepts are by definition not capable of being directly reduced to observable events or characteristics, we must then develop *indicators* of these concepts that are grounded in the empirical world and that may, as a result, be measured. It is through such indicators that theories and hypotheses may be tested against concrete data. Hypotheses that contain concepts for which we do not provide empirical indicators must remain as untested speculations. The development of adequate empirical indicators thus provides a crucial link in the social research process. But specifying such indicators is not always a simple matter. To return once more to the ideology example, several *conceptual definitions* may be offered. For example, political ideology may be defined as the global outlook of an individual toward the political world. Someone else might define it less generally as the set of beliefs about the extent of the government's role in solving societal problems. Presumably, each of these definitions of ideology would require different indicators (or operational definitions) to provide a test of the hypotheses. Focusing only on the second definition, several alternative indicators may be suggested. The scale made up of policy questions discussed above certainly seems appropriate, as would a single question on the role of the federal government in solving problems or an item asking respondents to place themselves on a scale ranging from strongly conservative to strongly liberal. The point to be made is that selecting an appropriate indicator for any particular concept is far from a purely logical exercise.

We thus come to the conclusion that besides the explicit theories or hypotheses we form to explain the phenomenon under study, there is a second, often implicit theory that is required to test it. Blalock (1968) has termed the latter *auxiliary theory*. Its function is to specify the relationships between the theoretical and empirical worlds or, more precisely, between abstract concepts and their indicators. These relationships have been referred to in various ways in the philosophy of science, sociological, and psychometric literature: epistemic correlations, rules of correspondence, and operational definitions, among others. These *epistemic correlations,* as we shall refer to them from now on, provide the basis for specifying indicators and testing our abstract hypotheses.

A convenient way of representing a series of abstract hypotheses along with the auxiliary theory necessary to specify the relationships between indicators and concepts is through the use of a causal model or diagram (Asher, 1976; Duncan, 1975a; Blalock, 1964). In such a diagram, arrows are used to indicate the assumed direction of causal relationships between variables—arrows pointing from cause to effect.[1] An example of this is shown in Figure 1: X, Y, and Z represent the abstract concepts in this simple "theory" which is an elaboration of a relationship between X and Z. The indicators used to empirically test the theory are $x_1$, $y_1$, $y_2$, and $z_1$. In this example, both X and Z have a single indicator each, while two indicators have been specified for Y. This should become clearer with a substantive example. Suppose one is interested in studying the relationship betwen age and attitudes toward captial punishment. Someone then suggests that a more general ideology of conservativism is an intervening variable accounting for the relationship. X is thus age, Y conservatism, and Z attitudes toward capital punishment. The data to test this could be collected through a survey of the appropriate population. The indicator for age is simple self-report. For attitude toward capital punishment the respondents are asked to place themselves on a scale ranging from strongly opposed to strongly in favor. Two indicators are used, however, to measure the intervening concept, ideology. $y_1$ is the individual's self-placement on a continuum from very conservative to very liberal, while $y_2$ is the scale made up of attitudes toward public policy issues.

In a straightforward manner we have thus represented simultaneously in diagram form both the substantive theory (hypothesis) we wish to investigate and the auxiliary theory developed to test it. In Figure 1, then, the horizontal arrows represent the relationships among the concepts that make up the substantive theory, and the vertical arrows indicate the epistemic correlations between the concepts and indicators that make up the auxiliary theory. As shown, however, this auxiliary theory is quite simple; it assumes that there are no other factors affecting the indicators other than the theoretical constructs. In the substantive example used here, this assumption seems to vary in its plausibility across the indicators used. We

12

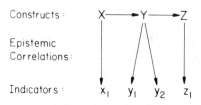

In one example, X = age, Y = conservatism, and Z = attitudes toward capital punishment

---

Figure 1: **Representation of an Abstract Hypothesis and an Auxiliary Theory Using a Causal Diagram**

would probably have little trouble with self-report of age as an indicator for the concept since we expect most people would give accurate answers when asked (even though this may not always be the case) and because the concept itself is already empirically grounded. We might have less faith in the other three indicators, especially for measures of such abstract concepts as ideology. At an intuitive level it seems clear that there are many problems that could develop when trying to choose good indicators. Researchers working in the field of measurement theory, especially psychometricians (Nunnally, 1976; Lord and Novick, 1968), have formalized such problems and classified them into two general categories.

The first source of outside influence on indicators is the introduction of nonsystematic or *random measurement error*. This is known as the problem of reliability. The important characteristic of unreliability is that the disturbing influence in the indicator is purely random or chance variation. The magnitude of such error can be shown clearly in the context of a causal model of the auxiliary theory such as Figure 1 by first assuming all the variables are standardized, i.e., have a mean of zero and a standard deviation of one. In this manner the magnitude of the epistemic correlations may be interpreted as a standard correlation coefficient. Since we are working with standardized variables (and assuming linear relationships), squaring the epistemic correlation gives the percentage of the variance in the indicator accounted for by the concept. If there are no sources of variation in the indicator other than the concept itself, the epistemic correlation linking the two would equal one since the concept was explaining 100% of the variation in the indicator. If random measurement error is added or the indicator becomes unreliable, the epistemic correlation will decrease correspondingly due to this other source of variation. The higher the correlation, then, the more reliable the specific indicator. Since the traditional reliability coefficient in the psychometric literature is defined as the proportion of the variance in the indicator accounted for by the abstract concept, or "true scores" (Nunnally, 1976), the epistemic correlation is simply the square root of the more common reliability coefficient. The two perspectives thus lead to essentially the same result but in different forms.

What are the sources of unreliability, or random measurement error? First, it is important to recognize that no measurement is ever error free. The use of a simple balance to measure mass, for example, may be affected by friction, imperfections in the mechanism, and errors in reading the scale, among others. Thus, there is no simple distinction between perfectly reliable and unreliable measures; it is the *degree* of unreliabity that distinguishes indicators. Random measurement error in the social sciences can emanate from any number of sources, too numerous to list (see Selltiz et al., 1976). A brief discussion of a few of these should serve to illustrate the larger problem. Random measurement error can arise from seemingly trivial sources such as errors in coding data from the original sources and subsequent keypunching mistakes. In survey research, questions or response categories may be ambiguous to the respondents. In this case, random errors may be generated as the respondents' judgments are affected by this ambiguity. Unreliability is not limited to survey reseach and may also be a factor in the type of data typically used in aggregate research. It is not difficult to imagine a number of simple accounting errors entering into the calculation of unemployment figures at the national level.

The important characteristic of these errors of measurement is that they are totally unsystematic. In the survey research example, an individual who is unsure between strongly agree and agree response categories is equally likely to choose each category upon repeated presentation (ignoring the influence of memory). If this error loses its random nature, the problem is no longer one of reliability but rather validity. The *validity* of an indicator is simply the extent to which it measures what the researcher claims it does: the theoretical concept. As soon as the error in our measures becomes systematic, some variation in the indicators is related to theoretical concepts other than the one it was designed to measure. Put another way, to the extent that an indicator is *reliable,* it contains systematic sources of variance. *Validity* is then the degree to which this systematic component is related to the abstract concept *as it was theoretically defined.* A reliable measure may thus be measuring (completely or in part) variables other than for what it was developed. Due to the nature of this source of error, it is sometimes labeled *nonrandom measurement error* to distinguish it from the problem of reliability.

Such a distinction is important since there are fundamental differences between reliability and validity not only in origin but also in their consequences for research and the appropriate techniques for dealing with them.

One way of illustrating this is by noting the relationship between reliability and validity: Reliability is necessary for validity but a reliable indicator need not be valid. Reliability is thus a necessary but insufficient basis for validity. As an example, assume that a researcher develops a measure that is defined by the height of an individual divided by twice the length of their left foot. Such a measure is likely to be highly reliable; assuming we have an accurate measure of length we should have no difficulty getting precise results with little random error. While reliable, we would consider it absurd if the researcher suggested this is an indicator of political ideology.

While showing the difference between reliability and validity, this particular example obscures another important point: the difficulty in determining the validity of an indicator. In the example it is obvious the indicator cannot be measuring ideology, but what about a more reasonable measure such as self-placement on a scale from very liberal to very conservative? This cannot be readily dismissed, but how can it be established as valid? This leads to another distinction between reliability and validity. The assumption that measurement error is random simplifies the task of estimating and correcting for unreliability. As will be seen, all that are required are some fairly simple assumptions and models. Validity is much more difficult to deal with since it involves the extent to which systematic sources of variance other than the theoretical concept are affecting the indicator. But the concepts are by defintion unobservable; it is therefore impossible to be certain that there is only a single source of systematic variance in the measure. In other words, there is no way to conclusively demonstrate that an indicator measures only what it was constructed to measure. The simple models for dealing with reliability therefore do not apply, and tests for validity depend on greater knowledge about the relationships between concepts. They thus require more complex models and elaborate tests. In addition, this also means that the validity of an indicator cannot be specified in as precise a manner as its reliability. While it is possible to express reliability in terms of the percent of random error in the indicator, there is no corresponding way to quantify validity in practice.

What are the implications of measurement problems for carrying out social research? As the framework discussed here shows, one cannot simply test theoretical hypotheses in isolation. Whenever hypotheses are tested, assumptions must be made about the indicators and the auxiliary theory linking them with the concepts. The failure to test these assumptions (i.e., the reliability and validity of the measures) can have a critical impact on the conclusions reached. A simple example will be useful here.

Figure 2 shows a model representing a test of the simplest hypotheses. This may in substance say that urbanization leads to political development, higher social status generates high job aspirations, or increasing age leads

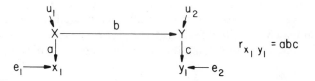

**Figure 2: Two-Concept, Two-Indicator Model**

to greater conservatism. X and Y are thus the theoretical concepts in the hypothesis we wish to test, and b is the structural parameter linking them. This parameter represents the magnitude of the relationship between X and Y (the concepts) in the population (see Appendix A). The indicators of the two concepts are $x_1$ and $y_1$, and a and c are the respective epistemic correlations. We shall assume that X, Y, $x_1$, and $y_1$ are all standardized. In testing the hypothesis we are interested in determining the magnitude of b: the strength of the relationship. In research, however, all we can measure is the correlation between the indicators $x_1$ and $y_1$: $r_{x_1 y_1}$. Since we have assumed that all the variables have been standardized, a, b, and c are path coefficients (Asher, 1976; Duncan, 1975a) and we can use the rules of path analysis to express $r_{x_1 y_1}$ in terms of the three parameters.[2] The result is the following equation:[3]

$$r_{x_1 y_1} = abc.$$

We would like to be able to come with a solution that would allow us to determine the magnitude of b. But the equation we have just written does not permit this since there are three unknowns (a, b, and c) and only one known quantity, $r_{x_1 y_1}$. In more technical terms the model in Figure 2 is underidentified (see Blalock, 1969; Fisher, 1966). The best that we can do is to express b in terms of one known and two unknowns:

$$b = r_{x_1 y_1}/ac.$$

While this does not tell us the exact value of b, it does produce some useful results. Since a and c are correlations they must be less than or equal to one. It is easy to see therefore that b must be greater than or equal to $r_{x_1 y_1}$. Furthermore, it will be equal to $r_{x_1 y_1}$ only if both a and c equal one, i.e., only if both are perfect indicators of the theoretical concepts. Only then will $r_{x_1 y_1}$ be an unbiased estimate of b. In any other case, it will underestimate the value of b.

The equation just derived to estimate the structural parameter may look more familiar when put in another form. The two parameters in the denominator are the epistemic correlations for the two concepts. Since they are equal to the square root of the traditional reliability coefficients, the equation may be rewritten in those terms. If we let $r_{xx}$ and $r_{yy}$ represent the reliability coefficients for each indicator, the above equation becomes:

$$b = r_{x1y1} \, / \, \sqrt{r_{xx}} \, \sqrt{r_{yy}}.$$

This can be recognized as the frequently seen formula for correction for attenuation. The auxiliary theory approach and psychometric theory thus produce the same result again. In this case, the explicit model makes the derivation much clearer.

The model we have been working with is obviously quite basic. The result derived from it, however, does apply to all other bivariate relationships; in the presence of *random* measurement error, the observed correlation is an underestimate of the structural parameter. In multivariate cases the situation is not this straightforward. Estimates are still biased, but they need not be always biased downward (Bohrnstedt and Carter, 1971). The most important rule that should be gained from this model is that with only a single indicator of each variable, there is no solution to the problem unless the researcher makes the unrealistic assumption of no measurement error in the indicators. In order to avoid such an assumption, more (empirical) information is required. This information can be obtained by increasing the number of indicators of each concept.

## VALIDITY, RELIABILITY,
## AND MULTIPLE INDICATORS

In the next sections, we shall discuss in some detail precisely how researchers can use multiple measures of abstract concepts in order to assess the validity and reliability of these measures. The most sophisticated analyses along these lines were begun by Campbell and Fiske (1959) on validity and by Costner (1969) and Blalock (1969) on reliability. In order to understand fully the presentation which follows, the reader should at least be familiar (if not facile) with classical measurement theory (Nunnally, 1976), path analysis, and correlation and regression analysis. We shall provide brief introductory comments on these topics, but the reader should have studied Asher (1976) carefully before undertaking this presentation.

As noted above, reliability refers to the extent to which an empirical indicator contains random measurement error. There are numerous approaches to assessing the reliability of measures, including test-retest correlations, measures of the internal consistency of items, and other methods based upon the analysis of multiple indicators, which we will cover in a later section.

Also as noted above, validity refers to whether or not one's empirical indicator measures the abstract concept that is used one's theory. This, of course, is somewhat vague, but perhaps the difference between reliability and validity can be highlighted by an example. Suppose the researcher is interested in testing a theory which produces the following hypothesis: in the United States, states which have more economic resources available will practice less economic discrimination against racial minorities.[4] The researcher's task is to first obtain operational measures of these two abstract concepts, economic resources and racial discrimination. If one could obtain the median income level for each of the 50 states, perhaps this could be used as a measure of economic resources. The reliability of this measure—median income—refers to the extent to which it contains systematic variation rather than random variation. In terms of Figure 2, how high is the epistemic correlation, a? The problem of validity, however, is more difficult. Assuming that there is considerable systematic variation in $x_1$, are we safe in assuming that the source of systematic variation, X, is the abstract concept in which we are most interested? In the current example, we could check the reliability of our measure by, for example, a test-retest method. We could obtain the median income, by state, at one point in time; and then a short time later (usually approximately two weeks), we could again obtain the median income for each of the 50 states. The correlation for median income at time one with median income at time two is an estimate of the reliability of the measure. Assuming it is high, we know that something is producing systematic variation in our measure, median income. We label that something X, in Figure 2. The problem of valdity is determining whether that X is truly the abstract concept we have in mind, economic resources. The source of systematic variation in $x_1$, median income, could be something else, such as resource development or the cost of living in the various states. If so, our measure is invalid. Unfortunately, there is no precise and simple way to determine the validity of our measure, but Campbell and Fiske's multitrait-multimethod approach is designed to help the researcher assess it as precisely as possible.

## Campbell and Fiske's Multitrait-Multimethod Matrix

In their classic article on the multitrait-multimethod approach, Campbell and Fiske conceptualize reliability and validity as follows:

> Reliability is the agreement between two efforts to measure the same trait through maximally similar methods. Validity is represented in

the agreement between two attempts to measure the same trait through maximally different methods. [Thus] a split-half reliability is a little more like a validity coefficient than is an immediate test-retest reliability, for the items are not quite identical [1959: 83].

This quotation is packed with important information, and it contains the rationale underlying their proposed methodology.

In classic measurement theory, one tries to gauge the *reliability* of a measure in a number of ways, but most of them involve some notion of repeatability. The test-retest correlation has been a common method of estimating reliability; it involves giving the same subjects the same measure (or test) at two different points in time, and then merely correlating the two sets of scores to assess the "reliability" of the measure in question. Here one assesses reliability in terms of "maximally similar methods"—in fact, by *identical* methods, merely at two different points in time. The split-half reliability of which Campbell and Fiske speak involves administering multiple measures of some trait, or abstract concept,[5] to be studied, and then giving all of these measures to the same subjects at the same time. One then merely correlates these measures with one another to assess reliabilty. Here, according to Campbell and Fiske's notions of reliability and validity, we are moving ever so slightly away from pure reliability (maximially similar methods) toward validity (maximally different methods). In most instances, the move will be so slight as to be undetectable, since the methods, while strictly speaking not identical, are often very similar. Thus we often devise two sets of questions to use on a questionnaire, both of which purport to measure the same trait. The precise questions used may differ, but the overall methodology—that of the interview—remains constant. Once we begin to move even further from the same methodology, we begin to approach the topic of validity, as conceptualized by Campbell and Fiske.

Campbell and Fiske introduce the notions of convergent and discriminant validity with reference to their definitions of reliability and validity. *Convergent validity* refers to their notion that if one's measures are valid, then even if one attempts to measure a trait, or abstract concept, by methods which are very different, the two very different methods ought to produce very similar results. That is, different measurement strategies should *converge* in the measurement of the same trait. *Discriminant validity* refers to their notion that if one's measures are valid, then these measures should *discriminate* among traits that are distinct. That is, even if we measure two different traits by the same method, our results should not correlate too highly because if they are different traits, validly measured, this difference will be reflected in our empirical results. Thus the correlation across different traits should not be too *large* or we might begin to suspect that our measures are invalid, perhaps due to some sort of methodological contamination.

Before examining these notions of convergent and discriminant validity in greater detail, we note the importance of some sort of validity assessment to the problem of generalizing from empirical indicators to abstract concepts, as discussed in our introductory section. In many respects, the problem of validity is the most critical problem in empirical research. (It is similar to the problem of "naming" or "labeling" factors in factor analysis.) Do the indicators measure the abstract concept of our theory? We *never* know for certain. It must remain somewhat problematic. However, Campbell and Fiske claim that we can at least be more or less confident depending upon some of the characteristics of our measures and how they relate to one another. If we claim to measure a certain trait, or abstract concept, with each of several very different methodologies, and these very different measurement procedures produce results which are quite similar, we may be *more* confident in the validity of our measures than if this were not the case. Quite simply, it is unlikely that such a pattern of results would occur fortuitously. If we can make a reasonable and convincing argument that each of several methods produces a valid measure of the trait or concept in question, and in fact each of these methods produces similar results, then we add credence to our claim of validity. This is the argument that Campbell and Fiske advanced. Of course, there are other methods for the assessment of validity, but they do not involve multiple indicators so centrally as the multitrait-multimethod matrix Campbell and Fiske proposed. The interested reader is referred to Nunnally (1976).

In the remainder of this paper, we shall examine four items of relevance to the Campbell-Fiske presentation. First, we will delineate precisely what the multitrait-multimethod matrix is and how it is used to examine measurement validity. Second, we will provide several examples of the method's application. Third, we will examine its significance in the broader context of research methodology. And fourth, in a later section, we will examine in some detail various criticisms of this particular methodology.

The requirements for a multitrait-multimethod (M-M) matrix are that we have at least two different traits each measured in at least two different ways, or methods. The traits could be anything—including attitudes, behaviors, and even the characteristics of aggregations rather than individuals, such as various characteristics of states, cities, organizations, and so on. The term *trait,* then, is essentially equivalent to the term *abstract concept* as we defined it earlier. The different methods, however, should be as dissimilar as possible.

Suppose we wish to study people's evaluations of the two major political parties in the United States. We could measure their evaluations by using an attitude questionnaire or an interview schedule. But suppose that one suspected that many respondents give a rather casual answer to our questions, answers which are often influenced by temporal and perhaps even random events. That is, one begins to suspect the validity of this particular measurement procedure. One could then attempt to measure, for some respondents at least, their partisan evaluation by somewhat different methodologies. For example, one could use the method of participant observation, spending two or three days with each respondent during a national election campaign, recording verbatim every conversational mention of either party. Then, one could record the number of positive and negative statements made by each respondent about each political party and arrive at a partisan evaluation as the net plus or minus value for each party. A third method would be to question each respondent's friends and relatives, using them as "informants" about respondents' partisan evaluations.

Now, further suppose that we used these same three methods to measure respondents' political ideology (liberal-moderate-conservative) and their degree of political involvement. Then we have measured three traits—partisan evaluation, political ideology, and political involvement—using three methods—interview with respondent, participant observation, and the use of informants. This would be a legitimate use of the M-M approach. If, however, we had merely included three sets of questions about each trait, on a single questionnaire, it becomes more questionable whether our application is appropriate. To be sure, we could use three sets of questions to measure partisan evaluation, and then perform a conventional reliability analysis of the results—because, as noted above, to the extent that these maximally similar methods (different questions on the same questionnaire) agree, this is evidence for reliability. However, the *method* is really one of an interview questionnaire, and although the content of the questions may differ, they will not differ enough to be validly called maximally different methods.

Let us grant, then, that we have met the preconditions for the M-M matrix. We have three traits measured three different ways. Table 1 illustrates this. Let the three methods be denoted as follows: 1 = interview, 2 = observation, and 3 = informant; the three traits are: A = partisan evaluation, B = political ideology, and C = political involvement. The data in the table are synthetic, and not data from a real study. They are meant only to illustrate the method. The entries in the table are correlation coefficients, and each correlation represents one of four different "kinds" of correlations. The first kind of correlation is that between two attempts to measure the same trait using the same method: the entries in cells A1-A1, B1-B1, C1-C1, A2-A2, and so on. These correlations are reliability coefficients, and may result from test-retest or split-half measurements, or a number of other methods. An example of the latter in the problem at hand would be using two different sets of questions in the interview schedule to measure partisan evaluation. The method is the same, although these specific questions differ slightly. There are many other methods to estimate these reliability coefficients, but they are beyond the scope of our presentation. All of the reliabilities in Table 1 are in the major diagonal, in parentheses.

The second kind of correlation in Table 1 is that between the same trait measured with different methods: the entries in cells A1-A2, A1-A3, A2-A3, B1-B2, and so on. Thus, they are represented by the diagonal entries which are located between the triangles formed by the dashed lines, and shall be called validity coefficients. They are called validity coefficients because they are the correlations among the same traits measured by maximally different methods, consistent with Campbell and Fiske's conceptualization of validity. In common sense terms, if we measure a trait several different ways and get about the same results no matter how we measure it, then our measurement procedures are probably valid to the extent they flow from our conceptualization of the substantive problem at hand. If our conceptualization of partisan evaluation leads us to the three very different types of measures discussed above, and if our results from these different measures are about the same, then we have strong evidence for validity. In assessing reliability, we examine the "repeatability" of our measures. If our measures reflect some sort of "methods variance"—if people give particular partisan evaluations partly because of the *interview situation* per se—then this methods variance will be constant as we assess reliability. In fact, it will *increase* our reliability, as it will produce stable responses. However, then we are measuring not only partisan evaluation but also partisan evaluation cum interview situation. For a measure to be valid, we want it to measure partisan evaluation but not the characteristics of the interview situation. If we have a high correlation between our different methods, we are probably not mainly measuring methods variance.

The third kind of correlation in Table 1 is that between different traits measured with the same method. These are the entries within the solid triangles: A1-B1, A1-C1, B1-C1, A2-B2, and so on. Campbell and Fiske call these triangles heterotrait-monomethod triangles, but we shall merely label the correlations therein as different-trait, same-method correlations. Finally, the fourth type of correlation is that between different traits measured with different methods. These are all the coefficients enclosed in the dashed triangles: A1-B2, A1-C2, A1-B3, A1-C3, and so on. We shall call these different-trait, different-method correlations.

**TABLE 1**
**Multitrait-Multimethod Matrix for Traits A, B, and C**
**and Methods 1, 2, and 3: Synthetic Data**

| Methods | | Interview 1 | | | Observation 2 | | | Informant 3 | | |
|---|---|---|---|---|---|---|---|---|---|---|
| | | A1 | B1 | C1 | A2 | B2 | C2 | A3 | B3 | C3 |
| 1. | A1 | (.82) | | | | | | | | |
| | B1 | .42 | (.79) | | | | | | | |
| | C1 | .38 | .33 | (.74) | | | | | | |
| 2. | A2 | .51 | .32 | .29 | (.69) | | | | | |
| | B2 | .31 | .45 | .19 | .44 | (.84) | | | | |
| | C2 | .30 | .25 | .39 | .38 | .32 | (.65) | | | |
| 3. | A3 | .58 | .31 | .30 | .62 | .36 | .28 | (.89) | | |
| | B3 | .35 | .48 | .21 | .25 | .68 | .25 | .46 | (.75) | |
| | C3 | .28 | .19 | .39 | .24 | .23 | .59 | .37 | .36 | (.68) |

Campbell and Fiske declare four criteria that the correlations in an M-M matrix should meet in order to stengthen the researcher's faith in the validity of his measures. The first is that the validity coefficients should be significantly different from zero and sufficiently large to encourage further examination of validity. For example, in Table 1 all of the validity coefficients are between .39 and .68. One should perform a simple test of significance for these correlations, to make certain they *are* significantly different from zero. If they are, one may then proceed to examine the other three criteria of the M-M correlations.

A second criterion of the correlations in the M-M matrix is that each validity coefficient should be larger than all different-trait, different-method correlations which are in the same row or column as the validity coefficient, and which are in the dashed triangles adjacent to the validity coefficient. For example, in Table 1 the validity coefficient for A1-A2 is .51. The relevant comparison, then, is between .51 and the coefficients which are in the same row or column as .51, in the two adjacent dashed triangles. These four coefficients are .32, .29, .31, and .30, all smaller than the relevant validity coefficient. The basic idea here is that the correlations *across methods* should be higher for the *same traits* than for *different traits*. Thus, party identification as measured by different methods should have more in common (more common variance) then party identification as measured by one method and political ideology as measured by a different method. If it does, this provides additional evidence of the validity of our measurement procedures.

A third criterion is that each validity coefficient should be larger than the coefficient between different-trait, same-method variables, which involve the same variable as that in the validity coefficient. For example, in Table 1 the validity coefficient for trait A1-A2 is .51, and this should be higher than the correlations in the solid triangles which involve A1 or A2 with other traits but with the same method. Thus, .51 is compared with the correlations between A1 and B1, A1 and C1, A2 and B2, and A2 and C2: .42, .38, .44, and .38, respectively. Therefore the criterion is met. The underlying reasoning is that, in general, for measures to be valid, there must be more trait variance than method variance, and thus measures of the same trait using different methods should correlate more highly than measures of different traits using the same methods. If the traits are truly conceptually distinct from one another, then most of their shared variance must reflect methodological variance.[6] The same traits measured with different methods should reflect primarily trait variance, and this trait variance should be higher than the methods variance of the different trait-same method correlations.

The fourth and last criterion for the correlations in the M-M matrix to reflect, if it is to be used as evidence of validity, is that the same pattern of correlations should be evidenced within each of the triangles (both solid and dashed) in Table 1. The solid triangles reflect correlations among different traits using the same method, while the dashed ones present correlations among different traits using different methods. Campbell and Fiske argue that the patterns in these triangles should all be the same. For example, in the upper solid triangle (which we shall reference as triangle 1-1), the pattern, in decreasing magnitude of correlations, is A1-B1 (.42), A1-C1 (.38), and B1-C1 (.33). This pattern of correlations should reflect the varous causal connections among the traits A, B, and C. All of the correlations ought to reflect some common methods variance, in this triangle, but the pattern of inequalities ought also to reflect the strength of the causal connections among the traits. Thus A and B are more highly related to one another than A and C or than B and C, according to the pattern in triangle 1-1 (see Note 6).

The first criterion is clearly met in these data. With a sample size of 26 or greater, the smallest correlation in the validity diagonal is statistically

**TABLE 2**
**Criterion Tests for Table 1 Synthetic Data**

*A. Criteria Two and Three*

| Validity Coefficient | | Criterion 2 Comparisons | Criterion 3 Comparisons |
|---|---|---|---|
| A1-A2 | .51 | .32, .29, .31, .30 | .42, .38, .44, .38 |
| B1-B2 | .45 | .32, .19, .31, .25 | .42, .33, .44, .32 |
| C1-C2 | .39 | .29, .19, .30, .25 | .38, .33, .38, .32 |
| A2-A3 | .62 | .36, .28, .25, .24 | .44, .38, .46, .37 |
| B2-B3 | .68 | .36, .25, .25, .23 | .44, .32, .46, .36 |
| C2-C3 | .59 | .28, .25, .24, .23 | .38, .32, .37, .36 |
| A1-A3 | .58 | .31, .30, .35, .28 | .42, .38, .46, .37 |
| B1-B3 | .48 | .31, .21, .35, .19 | .42, .33, .46, .36 |
| C1-C3 | .39 | .30, .21, .28, .19 | .38, .33, .37, .36 |

*B. Criterion Four*

| Triangle | Order |
|---|---|
| 1-1 (solid lines) | A1-B1 $>$ A1-C1 $>$ B1-C1 |
| 2-2 (solid lines) | A2-B2 $>$ A2-C2 $>$ B2-C2 |
| 3-3 (solid lines) | A3-B3 $>$ A3-C3 $>$ B3-C3 |
| 1-2 top (dashes) | A2-B1 $>$ A2-C1 $>$ B2-C1 |
| 1-2 bottom (dashes) | A1-B2 $>$ A1-C2 $>$ B1-C2 |
| 1-3 top (dashes) | A3-B1 $>$ A3-C1 $>$ B3-C1 |
| 1-3 bottom (dashes) | A1-B3 $>$ A1-C3 $>$ B1-C3 |
| 2-3 top (dashes) | A3-B2 $>$ A3-C2 $>$ B3-C2 |
| 2-3 bottom (dashes) | A2-B3 $>$ A2-C3 $>$ B2-C3 |

significant at the .05 level of significance. (See Henkel, 1976, for the test of significance and its assumptions.) The remaining three criteria are tested on the synthetic data in Table 1, and the results are presented in Table 2. In these artificial data, the correlations are constructed so that they all meet all of the criteria posited by Campbell and Fiske. In all cases, the criterion two and three comparisons are met in Table 2A, since the validity coefficient is always higher than all of the relevant different-trait, different-method and different-trait, same-method comparisons. Furthermore, the pattern is exactly the same within all of the triangles in Table 1—A and B evidence the highest correlations, A and C next, and B and C the smallest correlations. This is true regardless of the combination of methods involved in the comparison. Thus, as noted in Table 2B, criterion four is met as well.

Researchers could conclude from Tables 1 and 2 that their measurement procedures are most probably valid and that they have probably measured what they tried to measure. They could then proceed to examine and disentangle the relationships among these three traits, and perhaps between these traits and other, additional variables of interest. We have attempted to establish, by our application of the M-M approach, that our measures are valid, and this is prior to our attempt to address any substantive research questions. Once validity is reasonably established, then the substantive questions which interest the investigator must be addressed. Campbell and Fiske provide the criteria of convergent and discriminant validity to aid the researcher in this prior task.

It is undoubtedly true that, in most empirical situations, not all of the tests of Table 2 will be met by the data, even if the measures are valid ones. There will be some inconsistent patterns in the data, due to differing levels of reliability and validity and due to chance fluctuations in sampling of items and of subjects or respondents. The question of how close the data must be to the criteria proposed by Campbell and Fiske has not been answered clearly and concisely. One can perhaps get a feel for how various researchers have handled the problem by perusing the literature, but that is about all one can do. In the applications that follow, we hope to give the reader some feel for the problem and how it has been handled.

## An Application of the Multitrait-Multimethod Matrix to Achievement Motivation

Although much research has assumed that achievement is a unidimensional concept, Jackson et al. (1976) have subjected this assumption to an analysis via the M-M matrix. Their application is a bit unorthodox because they have not selected traits which are expected a priori to be uncorrelated (or only weakly correlated), but have attempted to specify several different types of one trait (achievement motivation), which may or may not be highly correlated. In their study using college students, Jackson et al. specified six types of achievement and utilized five different measurement strategies. We have selected three of each for purposes of illustration. The three types of achievement we selected are what they labeled (1) status with experts, which includes striving for expertise and acceptance of the judgments of experts, but not of nonexperts; (2) acquisitiveness, which includes material rewards as the primary achievement motivation; and (3) concern for excellence, which includes high standards of intellectual and cultural achievement. The three methods we selected include first, self-ratings, in which respondents rated themselves on a series of polar adjectives (three per trait). The second method, a simulation role selection, is an adaptation of Guetzkow and Cherryholmes's (1966) internation simulation, in which respondents were told that government representatives work best in posi-

**TABLE 3**
**Multitrait-Multimethod Application to Achievement Motivation**
**(based on Jackson et al., 1976)**

| Methods | | 1 | | | 2 | | | 3 | | |
|---|---|---|---|---|---|---|---|---|---|---|
| | | A1 | B1 | C1 | A2 | B2 | C2 | A3 | B3 | C3 |
| 1. | A1 | 1.0 | | | | | | | | |
| | B1 | –.16 | 1.0 | | | | | | | |
| | C1 | .42 | .07 | 1.0 | | | | | | |
| 2. | A2 | .30 | –.09 | .14 | 1.0 | | | | | |
| | B2 | –.05 | .34 | .28 | –.06 | 1.0 | | | | |
| | C2 | .15 | –.19 | .23 | .19 | –.04 | 1.0 | | | |
| 3. | A3 | .52 | .08 | .33 | .22 | .12 | .09 | 1.0 | | |
| | B3 | –.06 | .69 | .13 | –.10 | .38 | .20 | .17 | 1.0 | |
| | C3 | .40 | .02 | .67 | .11 | .27 | .18 | .35 | .22 | 1.0 |

Methods: 1 = self rating; 2 = simulation role selections; 3 = personality inventory.
Traits:  A = expertise achievement orientation; B = economic achievement orientation;
C = intellectual excellence motivation (see text for more details).

tions they themselves chose; the respondents were then given role descrip-tions, one for each trait, and asked to select one of these roles for the simulation; the title and description of the role were done carefully to re-flect only one of the traits. And finally, respondents took a personality inventory, with 38 items for each trait.

The correlations among these three traits and methods are listed in Table 3. The methods are quite different, but whether the traits are different enough to validate the measurement procedures is open to question. In fact, Jackson et al. did not use the M-M matrix to validate measures, but rather to examine the position that achievement motivation is unidimen-sional. They concluded that it was not, and we have selected three types of achievement motivation that are as different as possible. We shall examine the M-M matrix with validation in mind.

The validity coefficients in Table 3 are the correlations between the same trait-different method variables (diagonal entries between the dashed triangles). They range from .18 to .69. Campbell and Fiske's first criterion

**TABLE 4**
**Criterion Tests for Table 3 Achievement Data**

*A. Criterion Two and Three*

| Validity Coefficient | | Criterion 2 Comparisons | | | | Criterion 3 Comparisons | | | |
|---|---|---|---|---|---|---|---|---|---|
| A1-A2 | .30 | −.09, | .14, | −.05, | .15 | −.16, | .42,* | −.06, | .19 |
| B1-B2 | .34 | −.09, | −.19, | −.05, | .28 | −.16, | .07, | −.06, | −.04 |
| C1-C2 | .23 | .15, | −.19, | .14, | .28* | .42,* | .07, | .19, | −.04 |
| A2-A3 | .22 | .12, | .09, | −.10, | .11 | −.06, | .19, | .17, | .35* |
| B2-B3 | .38 | .12, | .27, | −.10, | −.20 | −.06, | −.04, | .17, | .22 |
| C2-C3 | .18 | .11, | .27,* | .09, | −.20* | .19,* | −.04, | .35,* | .22* |
| A1-A3 | .52 | .08, | .33, | −.06, | .40 | −.16, | .42, | .17, | .35 |
| B1-B3 | .69 | .08, | .02, | −.06, | .13 | −.16, | .07, | .17, | .22 |
| C1-C3 | .67 | .40, | .02, | .33, | .13 | .42, | .07, | .35, | .22 |

*B. Criterion Four*

| Triangle | Order |
|---|---|
| 1-1 (solid lines) | A1-C1 > B1-C1 > A1-B1 |
| 2-2 (solid lines) | A2-C2 > B2-C2 > A2-B2 |
| 3-3 (solid lines) | A3-C3 > B3-C3 > A3-B3 |
| 1-2 top (dashes) | B2-C1 > A2-C1 > A2-B1** |
| 1-2 bottom (dashes) | A1-C2 > A1-B2 > B1-C2** |
| 1-3 top (dashes) | A3-C3 > B3-C1 > A3-B1 |
| 1-3 bottom (dashes) | A1-C3 > B1-C3 > A1-B3 |
| 2-3 top (dashes) | A3-B2 > A3-C2 > B3-C2** |
| 2-3 bottom (dashes) | B2-C3 > A2-C3 > A2-B3** |

*Correlation larger than validity coefficient.
**Order incorrect.

is that these validity coefficients should be large enough. Here, with an N of 155, they are all statistically significant, although the reader should notice that the second method, the simulation role selection methods, results in much lower validity coefficients than the other two methods. This is because it is the most different method, since both the self-rating and the personality inventory require the subjects to describe themselves whereas the role selection is somewhat more of a behavioral measure.

The second criterion is that each validity coefficient should be larger than all of the different-trait, different-method correlations which are in the same row or column as the validity coefficient, in the adjacent dashed triangles. These comparisons are presented in Table 4. Fully 33 of the 36 comparisons are met, with only 3 of the different-trait, different-method correlations being larger than their corresponding validity coefficients. (All three exceptions involve method two). We would conclude that this criterion is met closely enough, although our guard ought to be raised.

The third criterion is that each validity coefficient should be larger than the different-trait, same-method correlations which involve the same variable as the validity coefficient. These comparisons are also in Table 4, and here only 31 of 36 meet this criterion; again, all 5 of the violations occur with method two, particularly with methods two and three as they measure the third trait, intellectual excellence. Thus two of three violations of the second criterion and three of six violations of the third criterion involve this correlation. One begins to suspect the validity of the second method, particularly with reference to the third trait.

The fourth criterion is that the same pattern of correlations should be evidenced within each of the triangles. For five of the nine triangles, the first and third traits correlate most highly, the second and third next, and the first and second correlate most weakly. The inversions are generally off by only one order, yet they suggest that there is some interaction between methods and trait—that some methods might be better measures of some traits. On this basis, one would probably want to investigate the matter further and to conduct a more sophisticated analysis of the data. We shall explore more sophisticated methods later, but for now we note that most data sets will not fit the M-M criteria better than this example. Most will fit it much worse. On those grounds, one might merely conclude that, given the vagaries of sampling error and measurement error, the data in Table 4 fit the criteria well enough for the analyst to conclude that measures are generally valid and may be used in further analyses. Further, one would conclude that there is very little correlation between these different types of achievement motivation, other than methods covariance. Yet we shall argue later than much more can be done to handle the problems of measurement error and methods overlap. Before we can make this presentation clear, however, we must go through the application of path analysis to multiple indicators. We shall present an introduction to this topic in the next section.

## Costner's Multiple-Indicator Approach to Reliability Assessment

While Campbell and Fiske argue for the use of multiple indicators for purposes of validity assessment, Costner (1969) presents a multiple-indicator approach to the assessment of reliability. To introduce Costner's procedure, let us review some of our earlier discussion in the introduction to this volume. The basic question Costner addresses is one of measurement error. Since we cannot measure our concepts directly, we devise empirical indicators of them. Thus, if we *could* measure the abstract concept directly, this "true" measure would not correlate perfectly with our indicator. In classical measurement theory, one distinguishes between "true" scores and "observed" scores, and one is able to adjust the observed scores by making certain assumptions about the structure of the variables, thus obtaining a reliabilty coefficient. If one is able to compute reliabilities by conventional formulas (split-half, test-retest, internal consistency measures such as coefficient alpha, and so on), little can be gained from Costner's approach, at least in its simplest form.

In order to compute these more conventional reliability coefficients, one needs to be able to obtain the same measurement at least twice within a short interval of time or one needs to administer a test or attitude schedule composed of multiple items which can be divided into two "parallel tests" or one needs to have a fairly large number of "test items" which measure the same thing which can be subjected to an internal consistency analysis (an item analysis). In many instances in sociology, political science, economics, and anthropology, we are unable to compute conventional reliability coefficients. In fact, often the unit of analysis is some aggregation, such as cities, culture, nations, and various types of groups. In the example given earlier, if we wish to measure economic resources and racial discrimination in the United States, it is very unlikely that we could obtain test-retest, split-half, or internal consistency reliability coefficients. It would be difficult to obtain test-retest data because the Bureau of the Census only collects such data at infrequent intervals, and if the interval betwen data collection points is too great, the true scores will themselves change considerably and the lowered test-retest correlations will reflect not unreliability but this true change. Split-half and internal consistency coefficients would be difficult to obtain because median income is only one item and to calculate these reliability coefficients it is necessary to have more than one item, or test, administered. Nevertheless, we do need to somehow determine how reliable our measures are and to correct statistical estimates for unreliable measurements. Costner's approach allows us to get a handle on measurement error in such situations.

Recall for a moment our analysis of the model in Figure 2. We demonstrated that when only single indicators of the theoretical constructs in the model are used, the reliabilities of our measures (i.e., the squared epistemic correlations) could not be determined. Furthermore, although we can show that the observed correlation, $r_{x_1 y_1}$, will underestimate the actual correlation between constructs, $r_{XY}$, there is no way to assess the magnitude of the attenuation.

Assume, however, that we are able to obtain two indicators for both X and Y, as in Figure 3.[7] We also shall introduce explicitly into the model in

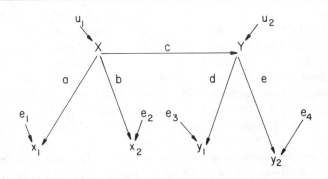

**Figure 3: Two-Concept, Four-Indicator Model with Random Error**

Figure 3 (and into all multiple-indicator models to be considered below) *error or disturbance terms,* to be denoted as $e_i$.[8] The error terms in Figure 3 will be assumed to be *random*; more precisely, this requires the following assumptions:

(1) $E(e_i) = 0$ for all $i = 1, \ldots, 4$ (i.e., all $e_i$ have a mean of zero)
(2) $E(e_i e_j) = 0$ for all $i, j = 1, \ldots, 4$ (i.e., the error terms are uncorrelated with each other).

Now, using the theory of path coefficients, we can write out all of the correlations among the indicators in Figure 3 as follows:

$$r_{x1x2} = ab \qquad [1]$$
$$r_{x1y1} = acd \qquad [2]$$
$$r_{x1y2} = ace \qquad [3]$$
$$r_{x2y1} = bcd \qquad [4]$$
$$r_{x2y2} = bce \qquad [5]$$
$$r_{y1y2} = de. \qquad [6]$$

Of course, the correlations in these six equations can be calculated given data for the indicators. Thus, we have a system of six equations with five unknowns (the path coefficients, a through e). Therefore, unlike the earlier situation in Figure 2, we can estimate c, the path coefficient (and correlation in this case) between true scores X and Y. To do this, we combine the information in Equations 1, 3, 5, and 6 to obtain:

$$c = \sqrt{c^2} = \sqrt{\frac{(acd)\ (bce)}{(ab)\ (de)}} = \sqrt{\frac{(r_{x1y1})\ (r_{x2y2})}{(r_{x1x2})\ (r_{y1y2})}} \qquad [7]$$

Thus, by taking advantage of the additional information provided by six observed correlation coefficients, one can overcome the presence of measurement error in one's indicators and correct for the attenuation due to random measurement error. The alert reader may have noted that we can also solve these equations for estimates of the epistemic correlations a, b, d, and e. This will be done later.

But the model in Figure 3 involves a system of six equations with five unknowns. This means that there is an excess of information and that not all sets of observed correlations among indicators will fit this model. More technically, we would say that the model of Figure 3 is *overidentified*. We can exploit this overidentification to test whether our data are consistent with the causal implications of the model, in particular the model's assumptions about the absence of nonrandom measurement error. From equations 2 and 5, we can see that:

$$(r_{x_1y_1}) (r_{x_2y_2}) = abc^2de.$$

Similarly Equations 3 and 4 imply that:

$$(r_{x_1y_2}) (r_{x_2y_1}) = abc^2de.$$

Therefore,

$$(r_{x_1y_1}) (r_{x_2y_2}) = (r_{x_1y_2}) (r_{x_2y_1}). \qquad [8]$$

Costner refers to Equation 8 as the *consistency criterion*.

If the causal process depicted in Figure 3 does indeed underlie the data, it is a *necessary* condition that the observed correlations satisfy Equation 8. If Equation 8 does not hold for a given set of data, the model in Figure 3 must be wrong. Often the model will be wrong because there is some non-random measurement error present, i.e., at least one indicator is affected by an extraneous variable apart from (1) the construct it represents and (2) its random error term.

Consider the model in Figure 4 which contains some nonrandom error between indicators $x_2$ and $y_1$. This model is expressed with the following set of six equations: Equations 1 to 3 as before; Equation 4a—$r_{x_2y_1} = bcd + fg$;

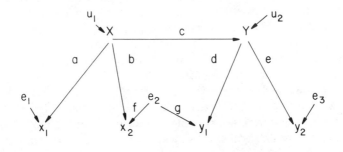

Figure 4: Two-Concept, Four-Indicator Model with Detectable Nonrandom Error

and Equations 5 and 6 as before. In this case we find that

$$(r_{x_1y_1})\,(r_{x_2y_2}) \neq (r_{x_1y_2})\,(r_{x_2y_1}) \tag{8a}$$

since $(r_{x_1y_1})\,(r_{x_2y_2}) = (acd)\,(bce) = abc^2de$

while $(r_{x_1y_2})\,(r_{x_2y_1}) = (ace)\,(bcd + fg) = abc^2de + acefg.$

Thus the left side of the inequality (Equation 8a) differs from the right-hand side by the quantity acefg. Unfortunately, in most practical circumstances, this additional quantity will be small, since it is the product of five paths, all of which will probably be considerably less than one. Thus it will often be difficult to tell whether, in any empirical situation, the two sides are slightly unequal due to sampling error or due to some nonrandom measurement error.[9]

It is useful at this point to recognize that in our earlier analysis of Figure 3, although we chose to solve only for the parameter c, the same equations can be solved to obtain estimates for the epistemic correlations—a, b, d, and e. Additionally, because the model is overidentified, there are going to be multiple estimates of these epistemic correlations, and indeed of the parameter c as well. It is possible to derive from Equations 1 to 6 the following pairs of estimates for each parameter in the model:

$$c = \sqrt{c^2} = \sqrt{\frac{(r_{x1y2})\,(r_{x2y1})}{(r_{x1x2})\,(r_{y1y2})}} = \sqrt{\frac{(r_{x1y1})\,(r_{x2y2})}{(r_{x1x2})\,(r_{y1y2})}} \qquad [7a]$$

$$a = \sqrt{a^2} = \sqrt{r_{x1x2}\frac{(r_{x1y2})}{(r_{x2y2})}} = \sqrt{r_{x1x2}\frac{(r_{x1y1})}{(r_{x2y1})}} \qquad [9]$$

$$b = \sqrt{b^2} = \sqrt{r_{x1x2}\frac{(r_{x2y2})}{(r_{x1y2})}} = \sqrt{r_{x1x2}\frac{(r_{x2y1})}{(r_{x1y1})}} \qquad [9a]$$

$$d = \sqrt{d^2} = \sqrt{r_{y1y2}\frac{(r_{x2y1})}{(r_{x2y2})}} = \sqrt{r_{y1y2}\frac{(r_{x1y1})}{(r_{x1y2})}} \qquad [10]$$

$$e = \sqrt{e^2} = \sqrt{r_{y1y2}\frac{(r_{x2y2})}{(r_{x2y1})}} = \sqrt{r_{y1y2}\frac{(r_{x1y2})}{(r_{x1y1})}} \qquad [10a]$$

In particular, we have obtained two estimates of $c = r_{XY}$. If the consistency criterion (Equation 8) holds *exactly* for a given set of data, both estimate expressions will give the same numerical result—a unique estimate of $c$. Just because of the presence of sampling error, however, we cannot expect Equation 8 to be exactly satisfied, even if nonrandom measurement error is completely absent. Thus we are typically faced with conflicting parameter estimates for $c$. If the conflict is small, an average of the two estimates can be used as a satisfactory estimate for $c$. If, on the other hand, the consistency criterion varies enough such that the two estimates of $c$ diverge considerably, one must assume that the model is indeed incorrect and begin to search for sources of nonrandom measurement error.

Unfortunately, Costner's consistency criterion is merely a necessary condition for the model to be correct. Even if the criterion is met (or approximately met within the range of sampling error), there are still several kinds of nonrandom measurement error which could be present. Figure 5 illustrates two of these. Figure 5a shows the situation in which there is

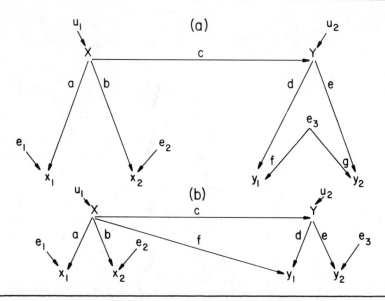

**Figure 5: Two-Concept, Four-Indicator Models with Undetectable Nonrandom Error**

within-set nonrandom error, likely for instance in questionnaire data if $y_1$ and $y_2$ happen to be contiguous questions. The equations defining the model in Figure 5a are Equations 1 to 5 as before and Equation 6b—$r_{y1y2} = de + fg$. But since Equation 6b does not enter into the consistency criterion, it will still be approximated. Figure 5b shows the situation in which one indicator is a function of both unmeasured constructs. This is most likely if the two constructs are highly related and are not entirely theoretically distinct. The equations corresponding to this model are:

Equation 1, as before

$$r_{x_1y_1} = acd + af. \tag{2b}$$

Equation 3, as before

$$r_{x_2y_1} = bcd + fb. \tag{4b}$$

Again, in this case, $(r_{x1y1})(r_{x2y2}) = (r_{x1y2})(r_{x2y1})$, since $(acd + af)(bce) = (ace)(bcd + bf)$.

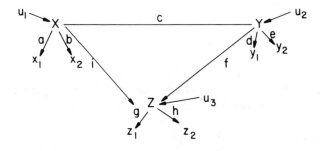

**Figure 6: Three-Concept, Six-Indicator Model with Random Error**

The consistency criterion is therefore not a sufficient condition for the absence of nonrandom measurement error, unless one can safely rule out nonrandom error between indicators of the same concept, and the presence of an indicator which is a product of more than one theoretical construct.

### Extensions to More Concepts

Costner's multiple-indicator approach can be extended to recursive models which involve more than two concepts, provided the causal structure remains the same (Blalock, 1969). In Figure 6, for instance, the top part of the model is the same as in Figure 3, and researchers can isolate that part of the model and analyze it in precisely the same fashion as they analyzed Figure 3. Thus, Equations 1 to 6 above hold for Figure 6.

In analyzing the relationships between X and Z and between Y and Z, the procedures are identical with the two concept case discussed above and the results will be the same, only the computations are a little more extensive. For example, in analyzing the relationship between X and Z we have:

$$r_{x_1 z_1} = aig + acfg$$

$$r_{x_1 z_2} = aih + acfh$$

$$r_{x_2 z_1} = big + bcfg$$

$$r_{x_2 z_2} = bih + bcfh$$

$$r_{z_1 z_2} = gh.$$

We can verify that an additional consistency criterion (identical to Equation 8 except that $z_i$'s will be substituted for the $y_i$'s) can be derived by noting that

$$(r_{x_1 z_1})(r_{x_2 z_2}) = (aig + acfg)(bih + bcfh) = abi^2 gh + abcfghi + abcfghi + abc^2 f^2 gh$$

and

$$(r_{x_1 z_2})(r_{x_2 z_1}) = (aih + acfh)(big + bcfg) = abi^2 gh + abcfghi + abcfghi + abc^2 f^2 gh.$$

The consistency criterion derived is thus:

$$(r_{x_1 z_1})(r_{x_2 z_2}) = (r_{x_1 z_2})(r_{x_2 z_1}) \qquad [8']$$

If we consider the relationship between Y and Z, we have the following equations:

$$r_{y_1 z_1} = dfg + dcig \qquad [16]$$

$$r_{y_1 z_2} = dfh + dcih \qquad [17]$$

$$r_{y_2 z_1} = efg + ecig \qquad [18]$$

$$r_{y_2 z_2} = efh + ecih. \qquad [19]$$

Similar logic then generates a third consistency criterion:

$$(r_{y_1 z_1})(r_{y_2 z_2}) = (r_{y_2 z_1})(r_{y_1 z_2}) \qquad [8'']$$

Thus, if the model in Figure 6 is correct and we have two indicators per construct, we have three separate consistency criteria that must be met: Equations 8, 8', and 8''. If all three of them are met within sampling error, then we can proceed to estimate the unknown path coefficients, in particular those between true scores.

But our estimation problem is somewhat more difficult now. We have a total of 15 equations (1-6, 11-19) and only 9 unknowns (a-i), so our system of equations is badly overidentified. This means that we will have multiple estimates of each unknown parameter, and if they differ very much we will not know which estimates to accept or reject. We could, of course, take some sort of weighted average, but as we shall show later, there is a better solution. For now, suppose that our three criteria are met and we wish to obtain some sort of corrected estimates for c, f, and i. Since the analysis of the X and Y relationship is the same as for Figure 3, we can estimate c just as we did before, using Equation 7. It remains to obtain estimates for i and f. First, we can obtain the following system of equations:

$$\frac{(r_{x_1 z_1})(r_{x_2 z_2})}{(r_{x_1 x_2})(r_{z_1 z_2})} = \frac{abi^2 gh + 2(abcfghi) + abc^2 f^2 gh}{(ab)\ (gh)} = i^2 + 2cfi + c^2 f^2 = $$

$$(i + cf)^2 \tag{20}$$

$$\frac{(r_{y_1 z_1})(r_{y_2 z_2})}{(r_{y_1 y_2})(r_{z_1 z_1})} = \frac{def^2 gh + 2cdefghi + c^2 dei^2 gh}{(de)\ (gh)} = f^2 + 2cfi + c^2 i^2 = $$

$$(f + ci)^2 \tag{21}$$

Now, since an estimate of c has already been calculated, we can treat c as a known in Equations 20 and 21. Then we have two equations with two unknowns (i and f) and, hence, can solve for i and f. Apart from estimating the parameters i, c, and f, we can also derive estimates of the true correlations—$r_{XY}$, $r_{XZ}$, and $r_{YZ}$. We need only apply the theory of path coefficients and trace paths in Figure 6 to obtain the following equations:

$$r_{XZ} = i + cf \tag{22}$$
$$r_{YZ} = f + ci \tag{23}$$
$$r_{XY} = c. \tag{24}$$

Then we can substitute our calculated values of i, c, and f into Equations 22 through 24 to derive estimates for the true score correlations. Of course, multiple estimates could be obtained for each of these coefficients. (We shall not pursue that here.) But if the three consistency criteria are approximately met, the different estimates should be quite similar.

The general point of this section is that Costner's simple consistency tests and his procedure for estimating the structural parameters in a simple bivariate case can be generalized to systems with larger numbers of variables. The extension to the four-, five-, or six-, and so on variable case is straightforward and is merely a generalization of the extension to the three-variable case. Every time we add a variable to the system, with at least two indicators per variable, we will increase the excess of equations over unknowns, and hence there will be a larger number of consistency criteria to be met and a larger number of estimates of each unknown parameter. The reader will have noticed that the algebra in the three-variable case, although simple and straightforward, leads to tedious computations. This is magnified considerably with each variable added to the system. For example, in the four-variable case, there will be 28 equations and 14 unknowns. The estimation problems thus become quite serious in complex systems of equations, and we advise the reader to use Costner's procedure only when the number of concepts is small and the estimation prcedures are thus simple. With more complex systems, we advise the reader to rely on maximum likelihood factor-analytic procedures.

### Extensions to More Indicators

Costner's approach can be generalized to cases in which there are more than two indicators per construct (see Figure 7). In such instances, there are nine consistency criteria:

$$(r_{x_1 y_1})(r_{x_2 y_2}) = (r_{x_1 y_2})(r_{x_2 y_1}) \tag{8}$$

$$(r_{x_3 y_1})(r_{x_2 y_2}) = (r_{x_3 y_2})(r_{x_2 y_1}) \tag{25}$$

$$(r_{x_1 y_1})(r_{x_3 y_2}) = (r_{x_1 y_2})(r_{x_3 y_1}) \tag{26}$$

$$(r_{x_1 y_3})(r_{x_2 y_2}) = (r_{x_1 y_2})(r_{x_2 y_3}) \tag{27}$$

$$(r_{x_3 y_3})(r_{x_2 y_2}) = (r_{x_3 y_2})(r_{x_2 y_3}) \tag{28}$$

$$(r_{x_1 y_3})(r_{x_2 y_2}) = (r_{x_1 y_2})(r_{x_3 y_3}) \tag{29}$$

$$(r_{x_1 y_1})(r_{x_2 y_3}) = (r_{x_1 y_3})(r_{x_2 y_1}) \tag{30}$$

$$(r_{x_3 y_1})(r_{x_2 y_3}) = (r_{x_3 y_3})(r_{x_2 y_1}) \tag{31}$$

$$(r_{x_1 y_1})(r_{x_3 y_3}) = (r_{x_1 y_3})(r_{x_3 y_1}). \tag{32}$$

The model represented in Figure 7 contains some nonrandom measurement error, but *if* it did not (i.e., if paths h and i were dropped and separate

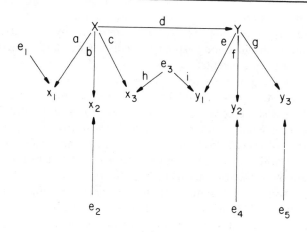

Figure 7: Costner's Two-Variable, Six-Indicator Model with Detectable Nonrandom
Error

error terms were added for $x_3$ and $y_1$), then all nine consistency criteria would be approximately met. The researcher could then conclude that, with the exceptions noted earlier, a random error model is most probably appropriate.

The advantage of using three or more indicators is primarily that of being able to pinpoint the source of the nonrandom error, should some exist. For example, if we posit the model in Figure 3 and test the consistency criterion (Equation 8) but it is not met, then we are unable to tell whether the nonrandom error exists between indicators $x_1$ and $y_1$, between $x_1$ and $y_2$, between $x_2$ and $y_1$, or between $x_2$ and $y_2$. If we had a theoretical reason to posit some nonrandom error structure a priori, then we could proceed to estimate c even if Equation 8 does not hold. For example, if we knew ahead of time that there was nonrandom error between $x_1$ and $y_1$, then we would know that Equation 2 does not hold. Since Equation 2 is used to derive Equation 7, we would be unable to use this estimate of c. However, Equation 2 is not used to derive the second estimate of c in Equation 7a, but rather equation 3 is used, so we could still estimate c by the second half of Equation 7a. We would be unable to test the accuracy of the model, but we could correct for attenuation in $r_{XY}$ by using this equation, *provided* we were certain the model was correct.

In most situations, unfortunately, we will not be in a position to posit such a model a priori with any degree of certainty. We will more likely hope that all error is random and then apply Equation 8, the consistency criterion. If this is not met, we know some nonrandom error exists, but we are uncertain of its exact nature. Thus we cannot test any particular model, and we cannot obtain a good estimate of c unless we have more than two indicators for each concept.

Suppose, for example, that we posit the model in Figure 7 without paths h and i; really, this posited model is wrong and the model in Figure 7 is correct (there is some nonrandom error between $x_3$ and $y_1$). Providing we have at least three indicators, we can discover the source of the problem. In this example, criteria 25, 26, 31, and 32 would not be met (since they involve the term $r_{x_3y_1}$), while 8, 27, 28, 29, and 30 would be met. Since the only correlation common to the four not met is $r_{x_3y_1}$, the researcher can (1) conclude that there is some source of nonrandom error between $x_3$ and $y_1$, (2) eliminate those two, and (3) proceed with the analysis. If all nine were met, there would then be nine estimates of c, all of which should be approximately equal. The point is simply that nonrandom error can often be eliminated if we have more than two indicators for at least some constructs.

If the consistency criteria are all approximately met, then we can simply keep all of the indicators and compute our multiple estimates of all unknown parameters, just as we did in the two-indicator case. In the three-indicator case, however, the excess equations over unknowns will increase much more rapidly thus leading to estimation problems even with a small number of variables. For example, in a three-indicator, three-concept model, there will be 12 unknowns but 36 equations. As a result, the major value of obtaining three indicators per concept is that of checking for nonrandom error. Once we have eliminated the inappropriate indicators from the system of equations, we can easily drop back to two indicators per concept and our estimation problem is more manageable, at least with small numbers of concepts.

## An Example Applying Costner's Procedures

Recall an example that we mentioned at the beginning of this section, about relating X = economic resources to Y = racial discrimination in the United States. Suppose we measured economic resources in the United States by $x_1$ = percent white collar and by $x_2$ = median income; and we measured racial discrimination by $y_1$ = discrimination ratio, computed by dividing black professionals' income by white professionals' income within each state, and $y_2$ = the same discrimination ratio for craftsmen. Then we can assume that the economic resources/discrimination hypothesis and our auxiliary theory are as in the model in Figure 2. We can compute all intercorrelations among indicators to obtain the information in Table 5.

Evaluated with these data, the consistency criterion, Equation 8, yields $(-.42)(-.75) = (-.57)(-.57)$ or $.3150 = .3249$, i.e., a difference of .01.

Later in this analysis, we shall present some tests of significance to aid in determining whether difference scores in the consistency criterion tests are likely to be merely sampling errors, but for the time being the difference in this instance between the two products is clearly quite small. Recalling that we are multiplying two correlations together, even if we take the square root of this quantity, we get only .1.

Since the consistency criterion is approximately satisfied, we would expect that the pair of estimates we can obtain for c using Equation 7a should be close. Indeed, we find the following:

$$c = \sqrt{c^2} = \sqrt{\frac{(-.57)(-.57)}{(.83)(.87)}} = \sqrt{.4499} = -.67$$

and

$$c = \sqrt{c^2} = \sqrt{\frac{(-.42)(-.75)}{(.83)(.87)}} = \sqrt{.4363} = -.66$$

The two estimates are within .01 of each other, so we have considerable confidence in our estimate of c and in the fit of the model in Figure 3 to our data set. Thus, in this example, we have been able to obtain an estimate of the correlation between true scores of resources and discrimination in the American States, an estimate which is better than the mere correlations among indicators. If the inequality of Equation 8 did *not* hold, then our two estimates of c would vary considerably, and, using Costner's procedure, we have no objective method to choose one or the other as the better estimate. Our best conclusion would be that the specified model is incorrect, i.e., does not fit the data at hand.

We should also note that since the consistency criterion is met using the data of Table 5, we could also solve for reliability coefficients for each of our four measures. Recalling the earlier discussion, we pointed out that the reliability coefficients are the squares of the path coefficients between true scores and indicators. So we can obtain esimates for the reliabilities by

### TABLE 5
### Correlations among Indicators of Resources and Discrimination
### in the American States

| | White Collar | Median Income | Disc. Prof. | Disc. Crft. |
|---|---|---|---|---|
| $X_1$ = percent white collar | | .83 | −.42 | −.57 |
| $X_2$ = median income | | | −.57 | −.75 |
| $Y_1$ = discrimination ratio, professionals | | | | .87 |
| $Y_2$ = discrimination ratio, craftsmen | | | | |

SOURCES: Percent white collar and median income are from *Congressional District Data Book 1963*; the two discrimination ratios are from Dye (1969).

using Equations 9 through 10a. For example, using the right-hand estimate of Equation 9, we have the following:

$$a^2 = \frac{(r_{x_1 x_2})(r_{x_1 y_1})}{r_{x_2 y_1}} = .6116.$$

Thus .62 is the reliability coefficient for the percentage white collar variable, and a value of .62 is not atypical. We could then use this reliability coefficient to correct for measurement error in further studies, although we would be taking quite a risk if the data set in this work were a different one.

In our example, however, it is impossible to tell whether the true model underlying the data in Table 5 is the model of Figure 3 or one of the nuisance models in Figure 5. Suppose, however, that instead of using percentage white collar occupations for our second indicator of resources, we used instead $x_2$ = per capita revenue. If we did use this, the relevant correlation matrix would be Table 6. Then, using Costner's consistency criterion, we would find the following:

$$(r_{x_1 y_1})(r_{x_2 y_2}) = (−.49)(−.75) = .3675$$

but

$$(r_{x_1 y_2})(r_{x_2 y_1}) = (−.54)(−.57) = .3078.$$

## TABLE 6
### Correlations among Indicators of Resources and Discrimination, Per Capita Revenue Replacing Percentage White Collar Occupation

|  | $x_1$ | $x_2$ | $y_1$ | $y_2$ |
|---|---|---|---|---|
| $x_1$ = per capita revenue* |  | .63 | −.49 | −.54 |
| $x_2$ = median income |  |  | −.57 | −.75 |
| $y_1$ = discrimination ratio, professionals |  |  |  | .87 |
| $y_2$ = discrimination ratio, craftsmen |  |  |  |  |

*The correlation between percent white collar and per capita revenue is .65.
SOURCES: Same as Table 5, and per capita revenue is from *Statistical Abstracts, 1963*.

And the difference between these two quantities is .0597 (the square root of the difference, analogous to a correlation coefficient is .24), considerably higher than that obtained using percentage white collar as an indicator rather than per capita revenue. In all likelihood, there is some sort of nonrandom error involved in the data in Table 6. Unfortunately, we are not able to determine precisely which indicators are affected by the nonrandom error. We could, of course, use theory and intuition to determine the nature of the nonrandom error. For example, we could posit that the correct model underlying the data in Table 6 is that represented in Figure 4. If so, we would still have more unknowns than knowns: six known correlations but seven unknown path coefficients. (In such a situation we say that the model is *underidentified*.) Fortunately, if we were certain that the model were correct, we could still estimate the value of c by using Equation 7, because the only correlation affected by the nonrandom error would be $r_{x_2y_1}$, and that correlation fails to appear in Equation 7. Thus, although we could not test the model or estimate all of its unknowns, we would still be able to obtain a unique estimate for the unknown correlation between X and Y.

Unfortunately, we will seldom be in a position to know that this particular nonrandom measurement model is the correct one. We will more likely begin from a position where we are unsure whether we have a purely random measurement model or one with some nonrandom error. We would then compute the consistency criterion and see how closely it is approximated. If it is not met, we then know that the random measurement model is incorrect, but we are unsure exactly which indicators are affected by the nonrandom error.

In the example at hand, we do not know precisely where the detectable nonrandom error lies among the indicators noted in Table 6. If we suspected that it was between median income and the discrimination ratio for professionals, our estimate of $c^2$ would be .51; whereas if we suspected that it was between median income and the discrimination ratio for craftsmen, it would be .41. So our estimate of the strength of the relationship between resources and discrimination would depend considerably upon which set of indicators we specified as subject to nonrandom error. Unless we know, a priori, we cannot be certain which estimate of c to accept. In fact, we would be merely guessing.

As we noted above, one way to get a handle on the problem is to work with three or more indicators. Suppose we work with all three indicators of economic resources at once. Then we have the model in Figure 8, which has three consistency criteria: as before,

$$(r_{x_1y_1})(r_{x_2y_2}) = (r_{x_1y_2})(r_{x_2y_1}). \qquad [8]$$

Then substituting $x_3$ for $x_1$ we get:

$$(r_{x_3y_1})(r_{x_2y_2}) = (r_{x_3y_2})(r_{x_2y_1}). \qquad [34]$$

Finally, substituting $x_3$ for $x_2$ in Equation 8 yields:

$$(r_{x_1y_1})(r_{x_3y_2}) = (r_{x_1y_2})(r_{x_3y_1}). \qquad [35]$$

We have already worked out Equation 8, and the two sides of the equality are .3150 and .3249, a difference of about .01; we also earlier worked out Equation 34, although we used different subscripts, and the two sides are

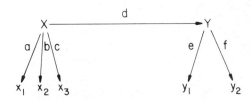

$x_1$ = percent white collar
$x_2$ = median income
$x_3$ = percapita revenue
$y_1$ = discrimination ratio, professionals
$y_2$ = discrimination ratio, craftsmen

Figure 8: Two-Variable, Five-Indicator Model for Resources and Discrimination

TABLE 7
Correlations among Indicators of Resources, Discrimination,
and Party Competition

| | $x_1$ | $x_2$ | $y_1$ | $y_2$ | $z_1$ | $z_2$ |
|---|---|---|---|---|---|---|
| $x_1$ = percent white collar | | .83 | −.42 | −.57 | .56 | .67 |
| $x_2$ = median income | | | −.57 | −.75 | .73 | .81 |
| $y_1$ = discrimination ratio, professionals | | | | .87 | −.67 | −.74 |
| $y_2$ = discrimination ratio, craftsmen | | | | | −.76 | −.83 |
| $z_1$ = Dawson and Robinson Index | | | | | | .94 |
| $z_2$ = Ranney Index | | | | | | |

SOURCES: Same as Table 5 and the Dawson and Robinson Index is from Dawson and Robinson (1953). The Ranney index is from Ranney (1965).

.3675 and .3078, a difference of almost .06; the third equality, Equation 35, had values of .227 on the right and .279 on the left, a difference of over .05 (data from Table 6). Recalling that these values are similar to squared correlations, the latter two differences are quite substantial, equivalent to correlations in the mid .20s. Equations 34 and 35 have two correlations in common which are missing in Equation 8: $r_{x3y1}$ and $r_{x1y2}$. The obvious culprit is $x_3$, which has nonrandom error with either $y_1$, $y_2$, or both of them. The solution would be to eliminate $x_3$ and work only with the other four indicators.

Suppose we add a third concept to our system, that of party competition in the American States. If we let Z = party competition, we might examine a model such as Figure 6, with both resources and discrimination affecting party competition (though in opposite directions). Let $z_1$ = the Dawson and Robinson (1963) index of interparty competition, and $z_2$ = the Ranney (1965) index; then the relevant correlation matrix is that shown in Table 7. Applying the consistency criterion we find that:

$$(r_{x_1 z_1}) (r_{x_2 z_2}) = (.56) (.81) = .4536$$

and

$$(r_{x_1 z_2}) (r_{x_2 z_1}) = (.67) (.73) = .4891.$$

Thus the difference between the two sides of Equation 8', in this example, is .0355 (and the square root is .18). For Equation 8'' we find:

$$(r_{y_1 z_1})(r_{y_2 z_2}) = (-.67)(-.83) = .5561$$

and

$$(r_{y_2 z_1})(r_{y_1 z_2}) = (-.76)(-.74) = .5624.$$

Thus the difference between the two sides of Equation 8'' is .0063 (the square root is .08). Both of these differences are quite small, particularly the latter. We might well conclude that the three consistency criteria are met, and if so, we can proceed to obtain estimates of c, i, f, $r_{XY}$, $r_{XZ}$, and $r_{YZ}$. First, using Equation 7 we get:

$$c = \sqrt{\frac{(-.42)(-.75)}{(.83)(.87)}} = \sqrt{.4362} = -.66.$$

(We use the negative square root of .4362 because of all four cross correlations between $x_i$ and $y_i$ are negative and because our theory tells us that resources will have a negative impact upon discrimination.) Then substituting for c in Equations 20 and 21 and taking square roots gives us the following:

$$\sqrt{\frac{(.56)(.81)}{(.83)(.94)}} = \sqrt{.5813} = .7624 = i - (.66)f \qquad [36]$$

$$\sqrt{\frac{(-.67)(-.83)}{(.87)(.94)}} = \sqrt{.6800} = .8246 = -[f - (.66)i]. \qquad [37]$$

(We use the positive square root of $[i + cf]^2$ in Equation 36 because we expect that $i + cf = r_{xz}$ is positive, and we use the negatives square root $[f + ci]^2$ in Equation 37 because we expect that $f + ci = r_{YZ}$ is negative.) From Equation 37 we know that $f = -.8246 + .66i$, and we can substitute this expression for f in Equation 36 to get:

$$.7624 = i - .66 [-.8246 + .66i] = i + .5442 - .4356i$$

Thus, $(.5644)i = .2182$, and $i = .39$. Substituting for i in Equation 36 gives: $.7624 = .39 - .66f$. Thus, $f = .3724/-.66 = -.56$. Now, having estimates of i, c, and f, we can use Equations 22 through 24 to obtain:

$$r_{XZ} = .39 + (-.66) (-.56) = .76$$
$$r_{YZ} = -.56 + (-.66) (.39) = -.82, \text{ and}$$
$$r_{XY} = -.66.$$

We have thus solved for the corrected correlations among the three variables, as well as the path coefficients among the true scores. And we see that the correlations among true scores are quite high; we also see that the direct impact of X on Z is much smaller than the direct impact of Y on Z (.39 versus −.56).

Since all of the consistency criteria were met closely in this case, we could generate a second set of estimates for the corrected correlations, using the equalities expressed in Equations 8, 8′, and 8″. If we did, our second set of estimates would be $r_{XZ} = .78$, $r_{YZ} = -.83$, and $r_{XY} = -.67$. These are almost identical with the first set, as we expect in this case.

In this section, we have presented Costner's procedure which uses multiple indicators to provide estimates of the reliability of these indicators, and in turn uses these reliabilities to correct our estimates of the parameters linking abstract unmeasured variables to one another. We have provided an example of the application of this procedure. We now return to the multitrait-multimethod matrix of Campbell and Fiske and use the method of path analysis to provide a critique of that matrix.

## CRITIQUE OF
## THE MULTITRAIT-MULTIMETHOD MATRIX

In a previous section we presented the Campbell and Fiske M-M matrix approach to the study of validity and discussed the criteria they suggest for interpreting the correlations in the matrix. We are now in a position to explore the usefulness of this technique in more detail by considering the model underlying the Campbell and Fiske matrix. We can do this by using the multiple-indicator technique to represent the various measures and abstract variables and then employing the principles

**TABLE 8**
**Correlations in a Two-Trait (X, Y), Two-Method (1, 2) Matrix**

| Methods | | 1 | | 2 | |
|---|---|---|---|---|---|
| | | $x_1$ | $y_1$ | $x_2$ | $y_2$ |
| 1. | $x_1$ | $(r_{x_1 x_1})$ | | | |
| | $y_1$ | $r_{y_1 x_1}$ | $(r_{y_1 y_1})$ | | |
| 2. | $x_2$ | $r_{x_1 x_2}$ | $r_{x_2 y_1}$ | $(r_{x_2 x_2})$ | |
| | $y_2$ | $r_{y_2 x_1}$ | $r_{y_2 y_1}$ | $r_{y_2 x_2}$ | $(r_{y_2 y_2})$ |

of path analysis to examine the structure of the relationships so generated. This will allow us to examine simultaneously the assumptions underlying this popular approach, and also to illustrate the extension of multiple-indicator models to more complex situations.

Our analysis will concentrate on the simplest M-M matrix—that with two traits each measured by two different methods—but our analysis can be generalized to larger numbers of traits and methods. The matrix for this case is shown in Table 8. Ignoring the reliability estimates along the diagonal, there are six observable correlations from the four distinct indicators, two traits and two methods. Each indicator is thus a combination of variation from two independent sources. This many be seen clearly in the formalization of the Campbell and Fisk model in Figure 9. The four indicators are $x_1$, $x_2$, $y_1$, and $y_2$, with the letters representing the traits and the numbers indicating the methods used. Thus, X and Y stand for the values of the two traits, while $F_1$ and $F_2$ represent the influence of the two methods employed. We further assume that there is some relationship between the two traits measured without error as shown by path S, and a similar correlation between the effects of the two methods, path R. In the latter case, we are allowing for the possibility that the influence of the two methods is in part similar. This would most likely be the case if the methods were two types of attitude measures on a questionnaire. Even more diverse methods may still be correlated if, for example, both involved a social desirability factor (Edwards, 1957).

An inspection of Figure 9 shows that there are 10 path coefficients or parameters to be estimated, but only six observed correlations (excluding the reliability coefficients in parentheses in Table 8). As specified, therefore, the model is underidentified (see Appendix A) and none of the paths can be estimated from the data. We can still make use of this represen-

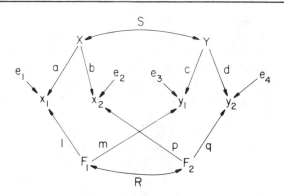

Figure 9: Causal Model of a Two-Trait, Two-Method Matrix

tation, however, since it is possible to express each of the correlations between the indicators in terms of the 10 path coefficients. This will in turn permit an examination of the criteria Campbell and Fiske suggest for utilizing these correlations to establish the convergent and discriminant validity of the measures. The following discussion is drawn largely from the work of Althauser and Heberlein (1970) and Althauser et al. (1971).

The 10 correlations in Table 8 represent the four different kinds of correlations discussed earlier. Leaving aside the 4 reliability coefficients, the remaining 6 may be expressed in terms of the parameters of the model as follows:

Same trait, different method (validity coefficients):

$$r_{x_1 x_2} = ab + lpR \qquad [38]$$

$$r_{y_1 y_2} = cd + mqR \qquad [39]$$

Different trait, Different method:

$$r_{x_1 y_2} = adS + lqR \qquad [40]$$

$$r_{x_2 y_1} = bcS + pmR \qquad [41]$$

Different trait, same method:

$$r_{x_1 y_1} = acS + lm \qquad [42]$$

$$r_{x_2 y_2} = bdS + pq. \qquad [43]$$

Campbell and Fiske's first criterion is that the validity coefficients be large and statistically significant. From Equations 38 and 39 it can be seen that these coefficients are a function of two distinct components. The validity coefficients may be large *either* because the epistemic correlations (a, b, c, and d) linking the true variable with the measures are large, as we desire, or because the method effects (l, m, p, and q) are strong and the methods are correlated. Thus, unless it can be assumed that the methods used are not correlated in any manner, the size of the validity coefficients will be exaggerated by methods variance, and even this most direct indication of validity will be misleading.

The second criterion involves comparisons between the validity coefficients and different-trait, different-method correlations in the same row and column as each validity coefficient; correlations across methods should be higher for the same traits than for different traits. The relationships underlying this comparison can be shown with one example—the second criterion's requirement that

$$r_{x_1 x_2} - r_{x_2 y_1} > 0.$$

Replacing these correlations by their equivalent expressions in terms of path coefficients from Equations 38 and 41, we find that the second criterion requires that

$$ab + lpR - (bcS + pmR) > 0$$

or, rearranging the terms, that

$$(ab - bcS) + (l - m)pR > 0. \qquad [44]$$

Again, this involves two components—the first a function of the substantive relationships (ab - bcS) and, the second, a function of method factors. Ideally, a large difference between these correlations should indicate that the two measures of X (in this case) have more in common across methods than measures of X with other variables. This difference should thus be primarily a function of the size of correlation S. And in fact, if a and c are approximately equal, the first term in equation 44 will be a function of S (or, more precisely, 1-S). But in order to conclude that this difference in correlations is simply a function of S, the second term must be approximately zero. This may occur in two ways. Either the method effects may be small (or the two methods uncorrelated) or the method effects may be quite large but approximately equal (l = m). In the latter case, a large difference in the correlations may still be obtained even with the presence of powerful method factors. In order to have any confidence in the results of this test for discriminant validity, it is thus necessary to assume away one of the major factors being examined, the existence of strong method factors.

The third criterion involves a similar comparison, this time between each validity coefficient and the different-trait, same-method correlations which involve the same variable as the validity coefficient. In this case we require that the correlation of two measures of the same trait across methods be higher than the correlation of measures of different traits by a single method, since if the latter is larger the measures will be more a function of method variance than trait variance. One example will again illustrate the logic underlying this comparison:

$$r_{x_1 x_2} - r_{x_1 y_1} > 0$$

$$\text{then, } (ab + lpR) - (acS + lm) > 0 \qquad [45]$$

$$\text{or } (ab - acS) + l(pR - m) > 0.$$

This is similar to the structure of the second criterion. In fact, if the assumption is made that b and c are approximately equal, the first term is again a function of (1−S) which is what we require. This will result in the first term being positive, its magnitude determined by the extent of the correlation between the traits.

The second term is different in this case since it is likely to be negative with a single path, m, subtracted from the product of paths p and R. Thus the size of the comparison between correlations will depend on the relative size of these two terms. If the method effects are strong, the second term will take on relatively large negative values and the overall difference between the correlations will be small. In other words, if the method variance is large with respect to trait variance, this criterion will be rejected. This is exactly what Campbell and Fiske intended. The third criterion therefore does seem to hold up under closer scrutiny. It is still necessary to assume, however, that the method paths are of like sign—i.e., that the methods influence the measures in the same way. And, for the comparison to be sensitive to methods variance, path S must be relatively small or the first term will not be large in the first place. Thus, if the traits are fairly highly correlated, even a relatively small degree of method variance may be overestimated.

The final criterion Campbell and Fiske suggest is a comparison of a different sort. This requires that the pattern of off-diagonal correlations in the same-method blocks be similar to the pattern in the different-method

**TABLE 9**
**Correlations in a Three-Trait (X, Y, Z), Two-Method (1, 2) Matrix**

| Method | | $x_1$ | $y_1$ | $z_1$ | $x_2$ | $y_2$ | $z_2$ |
|--------|---|-------|-------|-------|-------|-------|-------|
| | | *1* | | | *2* | | |
| 1. | $x_1$ | $(r_{x_1 x_1})$ | | | | | |
| | $y_1$ | $r_{y_1 x_1}$ | $(r_{y_1 y_1})$ | | | | |
| | $z_1$ | $r_{z_1 x_1}$ | $r_{z_1 y_1}$ | $(r_{z_1 z_1})$ | | | |
| | $x_2$ | $r_{x_2 x_1}$ | $r_{x_2 y_1}$ | $r_{x_2 z_1}$ | $(r_{x_2 x_2})$ | | |
| 2. | $y_2$ | $r_{y_2 x_1}$ | $r_{y_2 y_1}$ | $r_{y_2 z_1}$ | $r_{y_2 x_2}$ | $(r_{y_2 y_2})$ | |
| | $z_2$ | $r_{z_2 x_1}$ | $r_{z_2 y_1}$ | $r_{z_2 z_1}$ | $r_{z_2 x_2}$ | $r_{z_2 y_2}$ | $(r_{z_2 z_2})$ |

blocks. The traits should interrelate in a similar manner regardless of how they are measured. To examine this the matrix under consideration must be enlarged to include at least three traits, for example, X, Y, and Z. Such a matrix is shown in Table 9. In one example of such a comparison, an ideal result would be as follows:

$$r_{y_1 x_1} - r_{z_1 x_1} = r_{y_2 x_1} - r_{z_2 x_1}. \qquad [46]$$

Rather than presenting a new model for this enlarged matrix, the paths *to* $Z_1$ and $Z_2$ will be represented as the primes of the paths to $Y_1$ and $Y_2$. Thus:

$$r_{z_1 x_1} = ac'S' + lm'$$

$$r_{z_2 x_1} = ad'S' + lq'R$$

Using these along with the previously derived experssion for $r_{y_1 x_1}$ and $r_{y_2 x_1}$ gives the following ideal result:

$$(acS + lm) - (ac'S' + lm') = (adS + 1qR) - (ad'S' + lq'R') \qquad [46a]$$

Rearranging these terms produces:

$$a(Sc - S'c') + l(m - m') = aSd - S'd') + lR(q - q'). \qquad [46b]$$

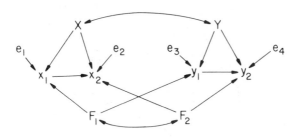

Figure 10: Model of a Two-Trait, Two-Method Matrix with Reactive Effects

Each side has two terms, one involving substantive relationships and the other involving method effects. The result is very similar to the analysis of the second criterion. It is possible for the equality to hold even if there is substantial method effects, if those method paths are approximately equal ($p = p'$, $q = q'$). Concluding from a consistent pattern of correlations that method effects are minimal is only correct, therefore, if the assumption is made that each method has a different magnitude of effect on each trait. Such an assumption cannot easily be justified and is, in fact, something for which we are testing.

This analysis of the Campbell and Fiske approach shows that only one of the four criteria they propose for establishing the convergent and discriminant validity of measures can be interpreted as they suggest without making heroic assumptions. And these have been arrived at on the basis of the fairly simple model in Figure 9. Figures 10 and 11 present slightly modified versions of this model that lead to even further complications.

One of the assumptions Campbell and Fiske implicitly made is that the measures of each trait are presented simultaneously. Since this is obviously an implausible situation on most studies, the problem of *reactivity* must be considered: the first measure of trait X may have a direct impact upon subsequent measures, independent of the true variable. This is the case shown in Figure 10. To the model in Figure 9, direct paths between $x_1$ and $x_2$ and between $y_1$ and $y_2$ have been added. This produces even further complications for the four criteria of validity. The most obvious example is for the first criterion of convergent validity. In this new situation, a high correlation between different measures of the same trait can be a result of (1) the measures having large epistemic correlations with

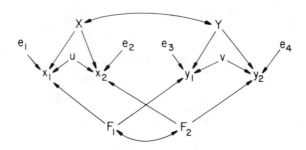

**Figure 11: Two-Trait, Two-Method Matrix with Correlated Error Terms**

the true variable, (2) a large correlation between method factors, or (3) a strong reactive effect of the first measure.

A second situation that leads to a similar result, but from a very different source, is diagramed in Figure 11. In this case, there is a second and distinct factor, besides the hypothesized trait, that directly accounts for part of the relationship between the measures. For example, two measures designed to tap political efficacy may also be influenced by an individual's level of political cynicism. Furthermore, in the model as shown, there is no way to distinguish between these two constructs. Even ignoring methods and reactive effects then, only a limited conclusion can be drawn from finding evidence of convergent and discriminant validity: The measures are tapping the same underlying trait. Whether or not that is *the* theoretical construct they were intended to measure is a question the Campbell and Fiske technique cannot completely answer and for which other strategies are appropriate (see, for example, Nunnally, 1976).

The multiple-indicator technique has proven quite useful in presenting the relationships underlying the Campbell and Fiske matrix and pointing out the strengths and weaknesses of the method. Unfortunately, even the basic model in Figure 9 is badly underidentified (see Appendix A) and, as a result, none of the substantive or method paths can be directly estimated from a real set of data. Althauser and Heberlein (1970) and Althauser et al. (1971) discuss certain approaches for detecting the presence of method effects in a two-trait, two-method model in the absence of full identification of the model. An alternative to this which allows for a full identification of all the parameters is the expansion of the matrix being examined. This can be achieved in two ways: either by increasing the number of traits or increasing the measures of each trait. Figures 12 and 13 detail two examples of M-M matrices that can be fully estimated.

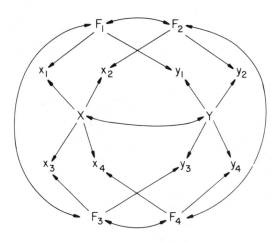

**Figure 12: Model of a Two-Trait, Four-Method Matrix**

In the model in Figure 12 there are still two traits being considered, but with four measures of each and thus four correlated method factors. There are 21 unknowns but 28 equations. Note that in order to identify this model, the number of indicators has been increased from two to four; a three-indicator model remains underidentified. If developing four distinct measures for two traits seems overly optimistic, Figure 13 provides a potentially workable alternative. Here, the number of measures has been reduced to two, while the number of traits considered is increased to four. There are 23 unknowns but 28 equations. If only two methods are available, it is thus possible to estimate their effects by employing them to measure four different traits.

Adding indicators or traits seems to provide a relatively simple way around the difficulties just described for the two-trait, two-method case: All of the relevant parameters may be estimated, providing direct information about the magnitude of methods variance. This information does not come without cost, however. As has been pointed out, adding more indicators or constructs to measurement models increases substantially the number of equations generated and frequently leads as well to multiple estimates of each parameter. The former creates computational difficulties while the latter leads to more significant estimation problems. Increasing the complexity of multiple-indicator models thus increases their flexibility in dealing with more realistic situations but limits the ability of these techniques to derive estimates of the parameters. We will return to this problem in the concluding section.

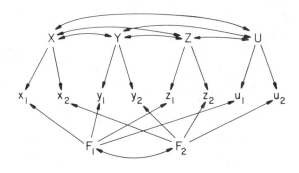

Figure 13: Model of a Four-Trait, Two-Method Matrix

## MULTIPLE-INDICATOR MODELS FOR PANEL DATA

The models we have discussed have stressed the utility of employing multiple indicators of unmeasured concepts as a way of dealing with the problems of reliability and validity. Up to now, this has been accomplished by specifying multiple measures of different constructs measured at roughly the same point in time. An alternative to such cross-sectional models is to utilize data collected at two or more temporally spaced points: *a panel design.* The simplest such design is the test-retest correlation discussed earlier as a basic model for assessing reliability. The logic behind this is that, with little or no random measurement error, repeated applications of a measurement instrument should produce identical or nearly identical results. Across a group of people, therefore, the correlation between the measure at two time points or waves should be very high. On the other hand, random error will reduce this over-time correspondence for each individual. The absence of a high correlation is taken, therefore, as an indication of unreliability.

Figure 14 shows a model of the test-retest situation. The unobserved variable, X, is measured at two distinct points by the same indicator x'. The subscripts represent the time period of measurement. To review, the paths marked a are the epistemic correlations linking the true variable with the indicator and are the square root of the reliability coefficient. We are thus assuming for the moment that the reliability of the measure, x', is constant over time. Path b represents the true stability of X over the period between measurements; it is the correlation that would be obtained

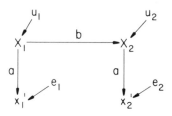

Figure 14: Model of a Test-Retest Correlation

if there were no measurement error. The resulting model is thus structurally equivalent to the model in Figure 2, analyzed earlier, with the exception of the assumed equality of the epistemic correlations.

The observed test-retest correlation may be expressed through the theory of path analysis as a function of the two parameters of the model. (Since the variables correlated are just repeated applications of the same instrument, we will simplify the notation in this section by using $r_{12}$ instead of $r_{x_1'x_2'}$.)

$$r_{12} = a^2 b. \qquad [47]$$

Since a is the square root of the reliability coefficient, $r_{x'x'}$, this may also be expressed as

$$r_{12} = r_{x'x'} b. \qquad [48]$$

In this form the problem with the test-retest correlation as an estimate of reliability becomes apparent: The correlation is an unbiased estimate of reliability only if it is assumed that the true variable is perfectly stable over this time period (i.e., b = 1). If any substantive change does take place, the correlation will underestimate the true reliability of the measure. Conversely, if one is interested in assessing the true stability of the variable, the measure must be assumed to be perfectly reliable if $r_{12}$ is to be used as an estimate of the stability. Furthermore, the model in Figure 14 is underidentified; no distinct estimates of a or b can be made from Equation 47. The parameters are thus completely confounded and inferences from this single correlation must be based on one of two risky assumptions.

While the two-wave, one-indicator case is an apparent dead-end, Heise (1971) has shown that adding a third time period will permit distinct estimates of the reliability and true stabilities if certain assumptions are made. The resulting three-wave, one-variable model is shown in

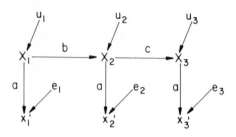

**Figure 15: Three-Wave, One-Indicator Model**

Figure 15. Here we have again assumed that the epistemic correlation, or reliability coefficient, for the indicator remains unchanged across the measurement period. Paths b and c represent the stability of the true variable over the first and second periods, respectively. According to the model, and from the basic theorem of path analysis, the stability from time one to time three is the product of b and c. There are now three observed correlations and three parameters to estimate; the model is, therefore, just identified and a single estimate for each parameter is possible. The three correlations may be expressed in terms of the three parameters of the model as follows:

$$r_{12} = aba = a^2b \qquad\qquad [49]$$

$$r_{23} = aca = a^2c \qquad\qquad [50]$$

$$r_{13} = abca = a^2bc. \qquad\qquad [51]$$

This yields three equations with three unknowns which may be manipulated quite easily to solve for a, b, and c. For example, the first two equations may be rearranged as follows:

$$b = r_{12}/a^2 \qquad\qquad [52]$$

$$c = r_{23}/a^2$$

Substituting these expressions for b and c into Equation 51 gives:

$$r_{13} = a^2 \cdot \frac{r_{12}}{a^2} \cdot \frac{r_{23}}{a^2} = \frac{r_{12}r_{23}}{a^2} . \quad [53]$$

Thus:

$$a = \sqrt{\frac{r_{12}r_{23}}{r_{13}}} . \quad [54]$$

Since the reliability coefficient is just the square of a, this leads directly to an estimate of the reliability of the measure, $r_{x'x'}$, free of the effects of temporal instability:

$$r_{x'x'} = \frac{r_{12}r_{23}}{r_{13}} . \quad [55]$$

With this as an estimate of reliability, it is possible to obtain estimates of the true stability of the variable over time, since in the presence of unreliability the observed correlation will be an underestimate of stability. One way to accomplish this would be to use the correction-for-attenuation procedure described in statistics and psychometric texts (see Nunally, 1976). Alternatively, these estimates may be derived directly from the model in the manner just described for the reliability coefficient. Letting s represent the stability of the true variable over the specified time interval, we obtain from Figure 15:

$$s_{12} = b$$
$$s_{23} = c \quad [56]$$
$$s_{13} = bc$$

Then,

$$s_{12} = b = r_{13}/r_{23}$$
$$s_{23} = c = r_{13}/r_{12} \quad [57]$$
$$s_{13} = bc = r_{13}^2/r_{12}r_{23} .$$

By making a few apparently simple assumptions, we have thus been able to overcome the problems inherent in the simple test-retest correlation and obtain estimates of the reliability of the measure and the temporal stability of the true scores. As with any model, however, the estimates are only as good as the assumptions made. And there is no way to avoid such assumptions: Without them no model can be indentified. In the present case several of the assumptions do appear questionable under closer examination. These can be shown, in turn, to have significant effects on the estimates. The complete set of this model's assumptions can be found in Heise (1971). The discussion here will be limited to two sets of assumptions.

The assumption of equal reliabilities across measurements has already been discussed as necessary for identification: If unequal reliabilities were permitted, there would be five parameters to estimate from only three correlations. While at first it seems quite reasonable to expect the reliability of a measure to remain constant, Wiley and Wiley (1971) argue that in many cases this is quite unlikely. To see why, it is necessary to look more closely at the meaning of reliability. We have already shown that the reliability coefficient is the square of the epistemic correlation. It may thus be interpreted as the proportion of the variance in the indicator accounted for by the true variable, or the ratio of the true score variance to the total variance, where the total variance of the indicator is the sum of true score variance and error variance. More precisely, if the auxiliary theory linking a concept X with an indicator x′ can be specified by

where e is a random error term, then the reliability of x′ may be expressed by

$$r_{x'x'} = \frac{\text{var}(X)}{\text{var}(X) + \text{var}(e)} .$$ [58]

Thus, it is possible for the reliability of an indicator to change without the error variance changing if there are changes in the true score variance. This could occur in various ways. For instance, one might use a measurement instrument in different populations which would be likely to have significantly different variances on the true scores. A more relevant example for the present discussion would be a variable whose variance, because of the social or political processes involved, increases or decreases consistently over time. When this is the case, the assumption of constant reliability is incorrect and the estimates from a model based on it are biased. (See Appendix A on bias.)

Since the three-wave, one-indicator model is underidentified if the reliabilities are allowed to vary across time, the problem would appear to be unsolvable. Wiley and Wiley have shown, however, that if unstandardized data (i.e., variances and covariances) are used in place of standardized correlation coefficients, it is possible to estimate the parameters of the model by assuming only constant error variance [var($e_1$) = var($e_2$) = var($e_3$)] for the indicators. When the parameters are converted back to path coefficients the reliabilities will not necessarily be equal since the variances of the true scores have been estimated separately for each measurement period. While in the most general cases even the assumption of equal error variance will probably be incorrect, it is clearly less restrictive since it is a function only of the measurement instrument and not of the true scores. The details of the structure of this model and the resulting formulae for reliability and stability are given in Appendix B. For an extended discussion of this approach, see Wiley and Wiley (1971) and Werts et al. (1971).

Besides the direct application to this panel model, the Wiley and Wiley analysis leads to a more general consideration in the development of multiple-indicator models. To this point, all of the models we have discussed have been developed and estimated using standardized variables, i.e., Pearson correlation coefficients. The implicit assumption has thus been that the final results would be the same regardless of whether the data were standardized before the analysis and computations or they were left unstandardized until the final calculation of the path coefficients. Until this particular model this assumption was correct; it would make no difference if the model was developed and estimated from standardized or unstandardized data. As the present model shows, however, there are cases in which this clearly does not hold. In general, the final results will differ if the model specifies an equality between two or more parameters. This will occur because a standardized parameter is a function of several unstandardized parameters. A correlation coefficient is obtained by dividing the covariance by the product of the standard deviations of the two variables; equal covariances will thus typically be associated with unequal correlations.

Blalock (1967) has discussed the problems in using standardized coefficients when comparing models *across* populations. This discussion shows that even within a single population, the decision on whether or not to standardize may be just as important. This will most frequently be the case for the analysis of panel data since this is when specifying equalities between parameters will be a feasible, and sometimes necessary, strategy for identifying the model.

While the assumption of equal reliabilities may be unrealistic, the effect on the parameter estimates of violating it is in many cases minor. It would take a rather substantial change in the true score variances before the estimates from the Heise and Wiley and Wiley models become appreciably different. There is another set of assumptions made in the model in Figure 15 that could have substantial effects on the results. These assumptions take the form of an absence of correlations of the error terms ($e_i$ and $u_i$) across the three waves of data. Specifically, we assume that (1) the $e_i$ are uncorrelated among themselves and (2) the $u_i$ are uncorrelated among themselves. Both of these assumptions are highly tenuous. In one case the model has assumed that the errors of measurement for the indicators (the $e_i$) are uncorrelated. This would require that the measurement errors be completely unrelated across time. Such errors are likely to include, however, factors such as general response sets and social desirability. Since the same measure is being used at each point, this would lead to a distinct correlation across the waves, as would simple recall if the time periods were short enough. In fact, any sort of method factor as discussed in the previous section is likely to be correlated over time. Figure 16 shows the revision of the Heise model to include correlated error terms, or, serial correlation.

Since the model was just identified to begin with, it clearly is not identified with the addition of these three correlations. Even if it is assumed

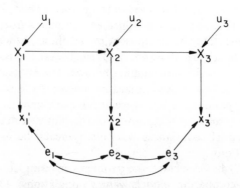

Figure 16: Three-Wave, One-Indicator Model with Correlated Errors

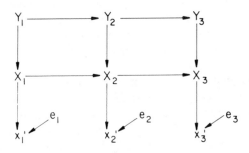

**Figure 17: Three-Wave, One-Indicator Model with a Persisting Disturbance Factor**

that they are all equal, the model remains underidentified. Furthermore, Heise has shown that the addition of more waves of data does not help the situation at all. There are always more unknowns than knowns. Thus, in the presence of correlated error terms, not only will the estimates from the model be biased but also there is no way the single-indicator model can be adapted to the situation.

In a second situation, the model has also assumed that the disturbances of the true scores ($u_i$) are uncorrelated. If the true stability of the variables is significantly less than one, this is also questionable. Here we are, in effect, assuming that whatever other factors determine the true scores at time t + 1 will be unrelated to the outside determinants at time t. But if any of these other variables are relatively stable, it is unlikely that they will cease to influence X over subsequent waves of the panel. Figure 17 shows one example of this with a second variable, Y (for simplicity assumed to be perfectly measured), affecting X over each wave of the panel.

If the model in Figure 17 is correct, the estimates derived from the model in Figure 15 will again be biased. As has been shown by Wheaton et al. (1977), such a misspecification can have a quite severe impact. In general, if the outside factor (Y in this case) is positively related to the variable being examined, the true stabilities will be overestimated and the reliabilities underestimated. The extent of the distortion introduced can be quite large due to another assumption of the model. This is because the model as developed initially is "lag-1"; $X_1$ can only have an impact on $X_3$ through $X_2$. This can be shown at a more intuitive level by noting that the model implies that the true stability from time one to time three is simply b times c (see Figure 15). In the presence of correlated errors, however, $s_{13}$ will be significantly larger than this product because of the

64

additional source of stability. In order to compensate for this, the model produces much larger estimates for b and c and, as a result, much smaller estimates for the reliability. Misspecification in this case is thus highly damaging due to the structure of the model. As was the case for the correlated measurement error terms, this version is also underidentified for any number of waves of data.

While no estimates can be secured from the models shown in Figures 16 and 17, Heise has provided a way of testing to see if these assumptions of uncorrelated errors are valid. This is possible if a fourth wave of data is added as in Figure 18. This model generates six observed correlations, and hence six equations are needed to specify the relationships between the path coefficients and correlations.[10] Since the model contains only four unknown path coefficients, it is overidentified. As a result, a consistency criterion can be derived (see Heise for the details of the derivation):

$$(r_{14}) \, (r_{23}) = (r_{13}) \, (r_{24}). \tag{59}$$

If the model in Figure 18 is correct, this equality should hold except for small differences due to sampling variation. If it does not, at least one of the assumptions is incorrect, and a different model is required to estimate the reliability of the indicators and the stability of the concept.

An alternative to the Heise model has been suggested by Blalock (1970; see also Namboodiri et al., 1975) and involves the use of multiple indicators of the underlying variable at two or more points in time. Figure 19 shows the simplest of such models, one structurally equivalent to the first Costner model we considered in Figure 3. For the present purpose, the two abstract variables are the same trait or concept measured at two points in time by the same two indicators. Path c is thus the true stability of the variable over the time period, and a, b, d, and e are the epistemic corre-

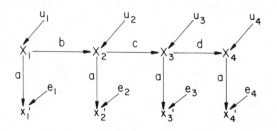

Figure 18: Four-Wave, One-Indicator Model

lations for the indicators at each point in time. There are several clear advantages of this approach over the single-indicator panel models just considered. First, estimates can be obtained from only two waves of data instead of the minimum of three needed for the one-indicator model. Because of this, the two-wave, two-indicator model is somewhat less sensitive to the effects of correlated disturbances. In fact, even if the $u_i$ are correlated, accurate estimates can still be obtained for the reliabilities.[11] This model also needs no restrictions on the values of any parameters in order to be identified; no assumptions need to be made, therefore, about equalities for reliabilities over time. It is even possible to explicitly test for equality in reliability over time. Finally, the consistency criterion for the two-indicator model provides a test of the assumptions of the model with just two waves of data, specifically a test for the presence of serially correlated error terms.

If the consistency criterion does indicate the presence of correlated errors, the two-indicator model of Figure 19 becomes inappropriate. Specifying correlations between $e_{11}$ and $e_{21}$ and between $e_{12}$ and $e_{22}$ would render the model underidentified. As the preceding section demonstrated, the flexibility of the model in dealing with such problems can be improved by increasing the number of indicators. This is illustrated quite nicely by the model in Figure 20. Here we are again dealing with the same concept at two points in time, but now measured by four indicators at each point. With the addition of two indicators it is possible to incorporate serial correlation into the measurement model without rendering the model untestable. In Figure 20, all of the parameters can be estimated, including the magnitude of the correlations between error terms for the same indicator at each point in time.

While this has succeeded in producing a measurement model that is more in accord with theoretical expectations—reliabilities are free to vary and the errors of measurement may be correlated—it does so at a

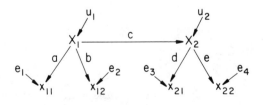

Figure 19: Two-Wave, Two-Indicator Model for Panel Data

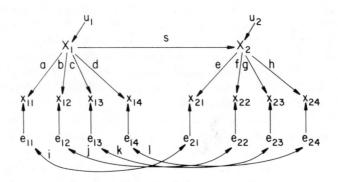

Figure 20: Two-Wave, Four-Indicator Model with Correlated Errors

price. This is the same problem encountered in the previous section; as the complexity of the model increases, the computations become more difficult and there are more conflicting parameter estimates to resolve. The path analytic techniques we have discussed here become inconvenient at best for dealing with models such as these. In the next section we will elaborate the nature of these problems and suggest an alternative estimation procedure.

Due to space limitations, this discussion of multiple-indicator models for panel data has touched on only some of the possible models and approaches. An extended analysis of the last models considered here can be found in Blalock (1970; see also Namboodiri et al., 1975). The problems involved in extending panel models of unobserved variables to more than one trait or concept are discussed by Duncan (1972, 1975b), Hannan et al. (1974), and Wheaton et al. (1977). A long and detailed analysis of various models for dealing with measurement error in panel data can be found in Joreskog and Sorbom (1977). Wheaton et al. and Joreskog and Sorbom, however, use estimation techniques more advanced than the procedures developed here.

## Applications to Panel Data of
## Party Identification and Attitudes
## Toward Political Parties

One of the most popular concepts in the political behavior literature has been party identification: The psychological attachment toward a political party. Much research has shown that, once formed, this attachment is relatively stable over long periods of time. The specific measure

**TABLE 10**
**Reliability and Stability Estimates for Party Identification, 1956-1960**

*A. Over Time Correlations*

| Party Identification Pairings | Observed Correlation | (Heise) True Stability | (Wiley-Wiley) True Stability |
|---|---|---|---|
| 1956-1958 | .843 | .948 | .950 |
| 1958-1960 | .871 | .980 | .981 |
| 1956-1960 | .826 | .930 | .932 |

*B. Reliabilities*

| | Heise | Wiley-Wiley |
|---|---|---|
| 1956 | .889 | .886 |
| 1958 | .889 | .889 |
| 1960 | .889 | .887 |

of party identification that was used in many of these studies, and is still in use today, was developed 20 years ago and has undergone virtually no changes since then. One question to deal with is whether the deviations from perfect stability observed in this measure are the result of changes in party identification or measurement error in the indicator. Asher (1974) has applied some of the models we have discussed in this section to the Survey Research Center 1956-1958-1960 panel data to separate the true stability of party identification from random measurement error.

The second column in part A of Table 10 gives the observed correlations for the party identification measure across the three waves of data. The correlations are certainly substantial but at the same time they are not perfect. For example, party identification in 1956 explains about 69% of the variation in the indicator in 1960. This could be indicative of significant levels of instability (true change). Columns 3 and 4 in part A give the results of applying the Heise and Wiley and Wiley models to these data (Figure 15 and Appendix B). There are two points to be made with respect to these estimates. First, in both cases the corrected stability coefficients represent significant increases over the correlations among the indicators and show evidence of very little change in party identification over this time period. Second, the estimates from these two models are almost identical; allowing the reliabilities to vary in the Wiley and Wiley model obviously had little effect. This can be seen clearly in part B of Table 10 where the reliability estimates for the two models have been provided. The estimates for the Heise model are obviously identical since they were so constrained. The differences among reliabilities in the Wiley and Wiley model, however, are barely visible even at the third decimal place. The assumption of equal reliabilities in this case therefore seems reasonable, and as a result the Heise model performed quite well and little was gained from the less restrictive Wiley and Wiley model.

The results of this analysis were not very startling because the uncorrected correlations for the party identification measure were so high in the first place. What would happen if evaluations of the parties, for example, were examined instead of psychological attachments? In this case more change over time would be expected and separating reliability from stability could be more critical. To see if this is so, data from another panel study, the Butler-Stokes investigation of political change in Britain, were used. A random half of the sample was asked a series of semantic differentials (Osgood et al., 1957) about each of the three major parties. Data are thus available for evaluations of the parties in 1963, 1966, and 1970.

Column 2 of Table 11 gives the observed correlations across the three waves of data for the semantic differential "good/bad" as applied to the Labour Party. These results are striking in comparison with the figures just reported for party identification (which are comparable in magnitude to those found in Britain). To determine whether this is due to changes in evaluations of the Labour Party or to measurement error, the Heise model was applied to these correlations. As seen in column 3, the results are dramatic. The stabilities are much closer to one, and the conclusion appears to be that much of the observed instability in this measure was due to measurement error. The estimate of reliability confirms this since it is only .378, a very poor reliability for an indicator.

Even though no test for the assumptions of this model can be performed (since there are only three waves of data), there is some reason to suspect the results. The semantic diffential is a frequently used technique for measuring evaluations of an object; it is difficult to believe it could be this unreliable. To test further, a second indicator, "foolish/wise," was added giving two indicators of evaluations of the Labour Party. These were then used in the model in Figure 19 to assess stability and reliability across two waves of data. In this case, the first indicator ($X_{11}$ and $X_{21}$) is foolish/wise and the second indicator ($X_{12}$ and $X_{22}$) is good/bad. Path c is the estimated true stability of evaluations of the Labour Party, while $a^2$ and $d^2$ are the reliabilities of foolish/wise and $b^2$ and $e^2$ are the reliabilities of good/bad.

Table 12 gives the results of this analysis for the three subpanels generated by the three waves of data: 1963-1966, 1966-1970, and 1963-1970. In each case, the consistency criterion is met quite well; none of the differ-

TABLE 11
Observed Correlations and Corrected Stabilities
for Labour Party Evaluations

| Panel Waves | Observed Correlations | True Stability (Heise) | |
|-------------|----------------------|------------------------|---|
| 1963-1966 | .359 | .950 | |
| 1966-1970 | .307 | .812 | $r_{xx} = .378$ |
| 1963-1970 | .291 | .771 | |

ences is large enough for concern. Below these tests are the estimates of the five parameters. (Since the differences in the consistency criterions are so small, only one of the pair of estimates is shown.)

The results from this model are clearly quite different from the Heise model (Figure 15) just examined. The average estimate for the reliability of good/bad is .637, which is much higher than the .378 value previously obtained. The average reliability for foolish/wise is somewhat lower at .480. Not only are the reliabilities larger, but as a result the estimated true stabilities are much lower. While they are certainly larger than the uncorrected correlations were, they indicate much more change in evaluations of the Labour Party than the Heise model would have led one to conclude. The results in Table 12 also provide a partial explanation for these vastly different estimates. Recall that the single-indicator panel model assumed that the true stability from time one to time three is the product of the two intervening periods. The model leading to Table 12 made no such assumption and may therefore be used to see how accurate that initial specification was. Since the stability estimates for 1963-1966 and 1966-1970 were .546 and .541, respectively, the stability for 1963-1970 should be .546 x .541 = .295 if the logic of the single-indicator model were correct. The true stability for 1963-1970 was estimated to be .462 and not .295 as required. The assumption was therefore incorrect and, as a result, the estimates were biased. In fact, the true stability over the full seven years is virtually the same as for the two shorter intervals. The problem in this case is obviously one of correlated disturbance terms (see Figure 17). Some relatively stable factor(s) is (are) affecting evaluations of the parties at each measurement. It is possible that attachments to the parties help determine party evluations over time and thus contribute to their stability. A more complete analysis would therefore require a panel model with at least two unobserved variables examined over time.

TABLE 12
Results of a Two-Indicator Panel Model of Labour Party Evaluations

| | 1963-1966 | 1966-1970 | 1963-1970 |
|---|---|---|---|
| $r(x_{11}x_{12})$ | .592 | .581 | .592 |
| $r(x_{11}x_{21})$ | .286 | .267 | .217 |
| $r(x_{11}x_{22})$ | .321 | .311 | .264 |
| $r(x_{12}x_{21})$ | .351 | .285 | .231 |
| $r(x_{12}x_{22})$ | .359 | .307 | .291 |
| $r(x_{21}x_{22})$ | .581 | .482 | .482 |
| | | | |
| | (.286) (.359) = | (.267) (.307) = | (.217) (.291) = |
| Consistency | (.321) (.351) | (.311) (.285) | (.264) (.231) |
| Criterion | .103 = .113 | .082 = .089 | .063 = .060 |
| | | | |
| c | .546 | .541 | .462 |
| $a^2$ | .482 | .544 | .537 |
| $b^2$ | .727 | .620 | .653 |
| $d^2$ | .518 | .414 | .383 |
| $e^2$ | .652 | .561 | .607 |

# CONCLUSIONS

## Hypothesis Testing

One of the advantages of multiple-indicator models that are over-identified is that the several estimates of each parameter provide a partial test of the assumptions of the model. The simplest example of this is in the two-variable, four-indicator model in which the single consistency criterion provides a check for some types of nonrandom measurement error. This criterion appears quite straightforward; if the model is correct, the difference between the two sides of the equation should be zero. If one side of the equation is much larger than the other, there must be a problem with at least one of the assumptions. But how large should this difference be before the model is rejected? This question becomes more difficult to answer if the correlations are derived from a sample of the population, since sampling variation alone could prevent the equality from holding. What we would like to know in this case is how likely it is that the consistency criterion holds exactly in the population given the deviations from equality found in the sample. The solution to this is to develop a test of statistical significance (see Henkel, 1976) for the consistency criterion.

Such a test does exist and in fact predates the development of these multiple-indicator models by several decades. This test can be applied to the present needs because of the similarity of the consistency criterion to the "tetrad difference" generated by a simple form of factor analysis. Working from this perspective, Spearman and Holzinger (1924) proposed an estimate for the standard error of this quantity which is just the difference between the two sides of the Costner consistency criterion. Thus, the tetrad difference, denoted by $t_d$, is defined for the two-variable, four-indicator model by

$$t_d = r_{x_1y_1}r_{x_2y_2} - r_{x_1y_2}r_{x_2y_1}.$$

The formula for the estimate of the standard error, S.E., is

$$\text{S.E.} = (K_1 - 2K_2 + 4K_3)/N + K_4/N^2$$

where:

$N$ = the size of sample

$K_1 = r^2_{x_1y_1} + r^2_{x_1y_2} + r^2_{x_2y_1} + r^2_{x_2y_2}$

$K_2 = r_{x_1x_2}r_{x_1y_1}r_{y_2y_1} + r_{x_1x_2}r_{x_1y_2}r_{x_2y_2} + r_{x_1y_1}r_{x_1y_2}r_{y_1y_2} + r_{x_2y_1}r_{x_2y_2}r_{y_1y_2}$

$K_3 = r_{x_1x_2}r_{x_1y_1}r_{x_2y_2}r_{y_1y_2}$

$K_4 = (1 - r^2_{x_1y_1})^2 (1 - r^2_{x_2y_2})^2 + (1 - r^2_{x_2y_1})^2 (1 - r^2_{x_1y_2})^2.$

This is obviously a cumbersome formula to calculate, and using it for a number of tests could be very time consuming. Fortunately, there is a simpler approximation that works well unless *both* N and the set of correlations are small. The formula for the approximation is $\text{S.E.} \simeq 2r(1 - r) / \sqrt{N}$, where $\bar{r}$ is the average of the four correlations in the consistency criterion.

Using either of these formulae as estimates of the standard error, it is possible to perform a simple t test to determine whether this tetrad difference is significantly different from zero (Henkel, 1976; Blalock, 1972). The t value is just the ratio of the tetrad difference to the standard error: $t = t_d/\text{S.E.}$ The significance level can then be determined by using a standard table for the t distribution with the appropriate degrees of freedom (N − 1), or by using a rule of thumb that for relatively large samples (N > 100), any ratio greater than two is significant at the .05 level. This provides a more precise basis for making decisions on model revision from the consistency criterion tests. If the difference is not statistically significant, it can be attributed to sampling error and not to a substantive problem with the model.

This can be illustrated best with an example from one of the models we have already analyzed. In the previous section several two-indicator panel models were used to determine the stability of evaluations of the British Labour Party. The results are in Table 12. In all three cases, the consistency criterion seemed to be met relatively well even though the equalities did not strictly hold. The significance test can now be calculated to see if this initial judgment was correct. Looking at the first of these models, the consistency criterion was found to be $(.286)(.359) = (.321)(.351)$ or $.103 = .113$. The resulting tetrad difference is thus .01. With a sample size of 600, the standard error for this difference is $2(.329)(1 - .329) / \sqrt{600} = .018$. The t value is therefore $.01/.018 = .556$. This value is clearly not large enough to reject the null hypothesis that there is no difference in the population. The initial decision on this model was thus correct; computation of the standard errors for the other two models in Table 12 yields exactly the same conclusion.

There is one other aspect of the consistency criterion test that yet needs to be discussed. Even with the availability of a test of significance, an incorrectly specified model may still go undetected if the observed correlations are small. This results because the consistency criterion involves a comparison of the products of two pairs of correlations. If the correlations are small, their products will be much smaller, and it will be unlikely that the differences obtained will be large enough to cause one to doubt the model. As a rule of thumb, Althauser et al. (1971) suggest that the consistency criterion will not be very discriminating with correlations among indicators of .3 or lower. An alternative in this case is to examine the different estimates of each parameter to see how much they vary. Even if the correlations are small, these estimates should be fairly close in magnitude if the model is correctly specified.

Another set of tests appropriate for simple multiple-indicator models has been developed by Mayer and Younger (1975) and should be mentioned here. These tests, based upon the canonical correlation model, have several advantages over the test just described. Mayer and Younger's method allows specific models to be compared, evaluates particular assumptions of the model, and provides a test of statistical significance for the correlation between the two abstract variables. Since the canonical correlation model has not been discussed here, and the mathematics linking it with the multiple-indicator models is beyond the scope of this paper, we will not present a detailed discussion of this set of tests. Those interested in this useful approach are directed to Mayer and Younger for a discussion of the logic and mechanics of their tests.

## Estimation

Suppose we are now convinced that the differences observed in the consistency criterion are due solely to sampling errors. There is still the problem that unless the tetrad difference is zero, the multiple estimates of each parameter will differ. These differences may be the result only of sampling errors and the model itself may be correctly specified, but the problem still remains. We would like to derive a single estimate of each parameter but the model yields several. In the two-variable, four-indicator model there are just two estimates to handle; this grows to nine estimates of the structural parameter in the three-indicator version and increases rapidly with the addition of more indicators or concepts. In the two-indicator panel model example just considered, the difference in the consistency criterion was found to be a nonsignificant .01. Even with such a good fit as this, the two estimates of the stability of Labour Party evaluations are .572 and .546. In other situations even larger discrepancies may be observed in models which pass the consistency criterion test. Clearly, it would be desirable to have some way of reconciling these alternative estimates.

One seemingly obvious way to solve this problem is to average the estimates derived for each parameter. This has been in fact suggested in various forms in the literature, either by just taking the average of each distinct estimate (Blalock, 1969), averaging the estimation equations to produce a single value (Duncan, 1972), or by otherwise adjusting the correlations so as to make the consistency criterion fit perfectly (Duncan, 1975b). Since each estimate from a properly specified model is theoretically unbiased, there is no reason to choose one over another and averaging would seem to be an appropriate procedure yielding an unbiased estimate (see Appendix A).

If the only criterion for judging an estimator were bias, this line of reasoning would be correct. There is, however, another aspect of an estimator to consider. As Appendix A indicates, we would like an estimator not only to be unbiased but also efficient. Efficient estimators generate greater levels of confidence since the sampling distribution of the estimates has a relatively small degree of variance. This means that the individual estimates from each sample tend to cluster closely around the true parameter value. (See Appendix A for a more detailed discussion.)

This provides a second perspective on reconciling multiple estimates of a parameter. While the averaging technique does lead to an unbiased estimate, Hauser and Goldberger (1971) have shown that it typically does not produce an efficient estimate. To see why this is true, they note that an efficient estimate in an overidentified model is a weighted average of the individual estimates. To achieve efficiency these weights should reflect the variability of the original estimates. When a simple average is taken, however, we are implicitly assigning equal weights to all of the estimates even though each of them probably had different variables. The result is thus an unbiased but inefficient estimate.

Since we typically do not have estimates of the variance of each of the parameter estimates, the situation would appear to be hopeless. In models that are not badly overidentified, this does not lead to very severe problems. If, for instance, the consistency criterion is not significantly different from zero, the two estimates in the two-variable, four-indicator model will usually not differ by very much, and any reasonable set of weights will not produce an estimate very far from the simple average. As the model becomes more complex and the number of estimates increases, a properly weighted average may be significantly different than the estimate derived from assigning equal weights. One solution in this case is to move from the path analytic methods that we have discussed here to a maximum likelihood approach to estimation (Hauser and Goldberger, 1971; Joreskog, 1969, 1973; Long, 1976).

While a detailed discussion of maximum likelihood estimation is beyond the scope of this paper, we can offer an intuitive description. To estimate the models that have been presented here, we have started with the observed correlations between the indicators and used the theory of path analysis to express them in terms of unknown paths. If the resulting equations are identified, it is possible to solve for each of the paths. Maximum likelihood estimation essentially reserves this procedure. Suppose a model is specified and values are assigned to each parameter. Starting with *these* as the knowns, it is possible to derive the correlations that would result from these estimates. The maximum likelihood programs use an iterative technique that basically readjusts the values of the parameters until the correlations generated approach the observed correlations as closely as possible. Single estimates thus result for each of the parameters of the model and the procedure guarantees them to be efficient. The technique also yields standard error estimates for each of the parameters and a chi-square test for the overall goodness of fit of the model.

## Multiple-Indicator Models: Some Final Considerations

Abstract concepts that are fundamentally unobservable provide a basis for much theory and research in the social sciences. This use of such variables in empirical analyses increases the problems of measurement error since abstract variables may be measured only indirectly. As some of the models in this paper have indicated, the effects of measurement error on the estimation of parameters linking such variables may often be substantial. This occurs whether one is examining cross-sectional relationships or the stability of variables over time. In either case, the influence of measurement error may be sufficient to alter the substantive conclusions of the research.

The same characteristic of these concepts that leads to the problem also helps to provide one solution. Abstract concepts can usually be measured indirectly not just by one but by a number of empirical indicators. It is the information gained from the relationships among these indicators that forms the basis for the measurement models discussed in this paper. When properly specified, such models allow estimates of relationships between concepts to be "corrected" for both random and nonrandom measurement error. This added information does not come without costs, however. First of all, certain assumptions must be made in order to derive estimates of the parameters. In the extreme case, in which everything is related to everything else, or all errors of measurement are correlated, the model will be underidentified and not useful in empirical research. Frequently some of these assumptions may be tested as is the case with Costner's consistency criterion. But even for this to occur other assumptions must be made *a priori* in order to produce an overidentifed model. While the necessity of making such assumptions may seem like a major drawback of the multiple-indicator approach, it is also one of its virtues since it at least requires that otherwise implicit assumptions be made explicit. Furthermore, in the absence of a multiple-indicator model (or some alternative technique), the researcher is making the more tenuous assumption of the complete absence of measurement error in the indicators.

A second set of problems has appeared at several points in this paper and has just been discussed in some detail: As a model grows more complex, the computations grow increasingly more difficult and the number of conflicting estimates of each parameter that must be reconciled increases. And the latter does not appear to have a simple solution within the path analytic framework. For those who believe that more complex models are closer approximations to reality, this result could be quite distressing. An alternative, of course, is to move to maximum likelihood estimation techniques in which even quite complex models may be tested provided they are identified. Such a recommendation should not be taken as an indication of a lack of utility of the models and estimation procedures discussed in this paper. In fact, in many cases these procedures can be very productive if a proper strategy is employed.

Since computation and estimation problems are minimized in the simpler models, the two-indicator model is most useful for estimating the relationships between the underlying variables. This is only possible, however, if those indicators are free from nonrandom measurement error. But this question is not adequately dealt with by the two-indicator model since the consistency criterion in this case is not sensitive to many types of nonrandom error. The three-indicator model is more appropriate for this task since it is more flexible in this regard; the multiple consistency criterion tests allow indicators contaminated with nonrandom error to be detected in a straightforward manner (see, for example, Costner and Schoenberg, 1973). If pairs of reliable and valid indicators can be found in this manner, they can be used to estimate the substantive parameters. This process makes use of a great deal of the information in the total set of indicators and at the same time minimizes the problems of computation and estimation. If, on the other hand, indicators free of nonrandom error cannot be found, the only solution is to move to more complex measurement models, and, as a result, possibly to other estimation procedures as well.

## APPENDIX A:
## SOME BASIC STATISTICAL CONCEPTS

### Populations and Samples

A *population* for any study is the total number of units or observations in which the investigator is interested. Some examples are all of the people who are residents of the United States, all of those people who are eligible to vote in the United States (the electorate), all of the newspapers currently published in France, and all of the currently constituted nations on Earth. Since in many cases it is either impractical or impossible to work with all of the units in the intended population, a *sample* is drawn. Most simply, a sample is a subset of the population. Because the sample is drawn to gain information about the entire population, the sample should be representative. This can be best achieved through the use of the principles of probability. A particularly important type of probability sample is a *random sample*.

### Parameters and Estimates

Our interest in populations and samples is in describing their characteristics. A *parameter* is a numerical characteristic of a population. For example, the mean income of all people in the United States, the percentage of the U.S. electorate under 30 who voted in the 1976 election, and the correlation between nations' expenditures for public welfare and their income distributions are all parameters of the relevant populations. Since we often do not have information on the entire population, the parameters cannot be computed directly. Instead, samples are used to derive *estimates* of the population parameter. This is done through the use of an *estimator*, which is a formula describing a procedure for guessing the value of a parameter. The specific result of an estimator in a particular sample is an estimate. The formula for a path coefficient in a measurement model is an estimator that has been derived to provide information about the corresponding population parameter.

## Bias and Efficiency

In the process of trying to estimate a population parameter from a sample, the problem of sampling error is introduced. Since a sample is only a subset of the population, there is a certain likelihood that it will not be perfectly representative. As a consequence, if we drew repeated samples from the same population and derived an estimate of the parameter from each of them, the estimates would vary somewhat. If this was done enough times, we could examine the distribution of these estimates. This yields a precise definition of what is meant by *bias*: If the mean of this distribution is equal to the value of the characteristic in the population, the estimator is *unbiased*. In practice, of course, we never calculate estimates from repeated sampling; we instead rely on theoretical *sampling distributions*. Thus, we know that in a correctly specified model, the path coefficient (which is a standardized regression coefficient) is an unbiased estimate of the population value.

Besides the mean of this sampling distribution, there is also the variability to consider. The estimates from these samples may cluster closely around the mean or the spread may be considerable. It would of course be desirable to have little variability since that would lead to greater confidence in a particular estimate. This property is known as efficiency: The unbiased estimate with the least sampling variability is termed "efficient." Efficiency is thus not an absolute criterion such as bias, but must be judged relative to all other estimators of that parameter. A more detailed, but readable discussion of sampling, estimates, and the properties of estimators can be found in Kmenta (1971).

## Identification

In any model there are a certain number of unknowns we wish to solve; these are the population parameters that need to be estimated. At the same time, there are a number of known quantities that can be directly calculated from the data: means, variances, and covariances (correlations). The *identification* problem is basically a question of whether there are enough of these known quantities to be able to solve for the unknown parameter. As a simple example, consider the following two equations:

$$3X + 4Y = 18 \qquad [A-1]$$

$$2X - 3Y = -5. \qquad [A-2]$$

In this case, there are two unknowns, X and Y, and two known quantities. These equations can be solved to find X = 2 and Y = 3. Such a system is said to be *just identified* since there is just enough information to derive a single estimate of each unknown.

The next two equations provide a clear contrast to this:

$$3X + 4Y + Z = 18 \qquad [A-3]$$

$$2X - 3Y + 3Z = -5. \qquad [A-4]$$

There are still only two knowns, but now the number of unknowns has been increased to three. It is impossible to solve for X, Y, and Z simultaneously using just the information in these two equations. If we specify a particular value for one of these unknowns, say Z, it would then be possible to solve for X and Y. But every different choice of values for Z would lead to a different solution for the equations. Such a system is said to be *underidentified*. There is not enough information to derive unambiguous estimates for the unknowns; in fact, an infinite number of solutions exist.

Finally, consider the following three equations:

$$3X + 4Y = 18 \qquad [A-5]$$

$$2X - 3Y = -5 \qquad [A-6]$$

$$X + 2Y = 10. \qquad [A-7]$$

This time there are three knowns but only two unknowns. It is therefore possible to solve for X and Y. With the extra information, however, it is now possible to solve for X and Y in three different ways since only a pair of equations is needed. Such a system is said to be overidentified; there is more information than needed to solve for the unknowns. These three distinct estimates need not be identical. Pairing Equations 5 and 6 gives X = 2 and Y = 3; Equations 5 and 7 yields X = -2 and Y = 4; Equations 6 and 7 yields X = 20/7 and Y = 25/7. Such inconsistent estimates from an overidentified system indicate an improperly specified model.

# APPENDIX B:

## THE WILEY AND WILEY THREE-WAVE, ONE-INDICATOR MODEL

The causal diagram for the Wiley and Wiley model is very much the same as the Heise model in Figure 15 except for certain changes that are necessary when going from a standardized to an unstandardized model.

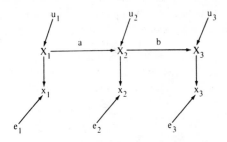

In this diagram, $X_i$ is the unobserved concept at time i, $x_i$ is the measured indicator, $e_i$ is the random measurement error, and $u_i$ is the random disturbance factor. The coefficients a and b represent the parameters linking the unobserved concept between times one and two and times two and three, respectively. Since the variables are no longer assumed to be standardized, these two coefficients can no longer be interpreted as path coefficients. They are essentially unstandardized regression coefficients relating the concept across time. From the diagram it is possible to write down three equations expressing the unobserved concept at each wave in terms of the disturbance terms and the two coefficients.

$$X_1 = u_1 \qquad\qquad\qquad [A-8]$$

$$X_2 = au_1 + u_2 \qquad\qquad\qquad [A-9]$$

$$X_3 = b(au_1 + u_2) + u_3. \qquad\qquad\qquad [A-10]$$

Similarly, the set of equations linking the indicators with the concepts is given by:

$$x_1 = X_1 + e_1 \qquad\qquad\qquad [A-11]$$

$$x_2 = X_2 + e_2 \qquad\qquad\qquad [A-12]$$

$$x_3 = X_3 + e_3. \qquad\qquad\qquad [A-13]$$

The terms in equations A-8, A-9, and A-10 can now be substituted into A-11, A-12, A-13 to yield:

$$x_1 = u_1 + e_1 \qquad [\text{A-14}]$$

$$x_2 = au_1 + u_2 + e_2 \qquad [\text{A-15}]$$

$$x_3 = b(au_1 + u_2) + u_3 + e_3. \qquad [\text{A-16}]$$

Since the variables have not been standardized, there are six observable characteristics of the indicators: the variance of each $V(x_1)$, $V(x_2)$, and $V(x_3)$; and three covariances, $C(x_1x_2)$, $C(x_1x_3)$, and $C(x_2x_3)$. If we make the assumption that $V(e_1) = V(e_2) = V(e_3) = V(e)$, these six variances and covariances can be expressed in terms of the model as follows (see Duncan, 1975: chapter 4, for a discussion on how this is done):

$$V(x_1) = V(u_1) + V(e)$$

$$V(x_2) = a^2 V(u_1) + V(u_2) + V(e)$$

$$V(x_3) = b^2 [a^2 V(u_1) + V(u_2)] + v(u_3) + V(e) \qquad [\text{A-17}]$$

$$c(x_1x_2) = aV(u_1)$$

$$c(x_1x_2) = abV(u_1)$$

$$c(x_2x_3) = b[a^2 V(u_1) + V(u_2)].$$

There are now six equations and six unknowns to be estimated: $a$, $b$, $V(e)$, $V(u_1)$, $V(u_2)$, and $V(u_3)$. The formulas for each of these may be derived from the equations in set 17 and are given below in the order in which they are derived.

$$b = c(x_1x_3)/c(x_1x_2)$$

$$V(e) = V(x_2) - [c(x_2x_3)/b] \qquad [\text{A-18}]$$

$$V(u_1) = V(x_1) - V(e)$$

$$a = c(x_1x_2)/V(u_1)$$

$$V(u_2) = V(x_2) - [ac(x_1x_2) + V(e)]$$

$$V(u_3) = V(x_3) - [bc(x_2x_3) + V(e)].$$

The reliability of the indicator at each point in time may be calculated from this since each reliability is just

$$r_{x_i x_i} = \frac{V(X_i)}{V(X_i) + V(e)} . \qquad \text{[A-18]}$$

Therefore:

$$r_{x_1 x_1} = \frac{V(u_1)}{V(u_1) + V(e)}$$

$$r_{x_2 x_2} = \frac{a^2 V(u_1) + V(u_2)}{a^2 V(u_1) + V(u_2) + V(e)} \qquad \text{[A-19]}$$

$$r_{x_3 x_3} = \frac{b^2 [a^2 V(u_1) + V(u_2)] + V(u_3)}{b^2 [a^2 V(u_1) + V(u_2)] + V(u_3) + V(e)} .$$

We still do not have estimates of the true stabilities, $s_{12}$, $s_{23}$, and $s_{13}$, since $a$ and $b$ are unstandardized regression coefficients. This can be remedied by noting that a path coefficient, $p_{12}$, is related to a regression coefficient, $b_{21}$, in the following way:

$$P_{12} = b_{21} \cdot \frac{\sqrt{V(X_1)}}{\sqrt{V(X_2)}} . \qquad \text{[A-20]}$$

Making the appropriate substitution for the variances of the unobserved constructs produces these estimates of the true stabilities:

$$S_{12} = a \frac{\sqrt{V(u_1)}}{\sqrt{a^2 V(u_1) + V(u_2)}}$$

$$S_{23} = b \frac{\sqrt{a^2 V(u_1) + V(u_2)}}{\sqrt{b^2 (a^2 V(u_1) + V(u_2) + V(u_3)}} \qquad \text{[A-21]}$$

$$S_{13} = ab \frac{\sqrt{V(u_1)}}{\sqrt{b^2 (a^2 V(u_1) + V(u_2) + V(u_3)}}$$

Note that as was the case for the standardized variant of this model, $s_{13} = s_{12} s_{23}$.

## NOTES

1. To be precise, causal diagrams—and the statistical techniques associated with them—have generally been reserved for models hypothesizing causal relationships assumed to be *linear*. Thus X → Y indicates that Y is generated by a causal process which can be represented by Y = BX + A where A and B are constants. When the variables are put into standardized form, this reduces to Y = BX since the means of each variable are set equal to zero. The models and prcedures discussed throughout this paper will be based on this assumption of linearity and also of interval levels of measurement. We should point out, however, that there is nothing sacred about these assumptions. In certain situations it would be quite plausible to work with ordinal variables or to hypothesize nonlinear relationships. At the present, however, multiple-indicator models relaxing these assumptions have not been pursued in any detailed fashion.

2. Recall that the theory of path coefficients allows one to write out the correlations between variables as a series of path coefficients. One may trace the paths between variables by going backward, or forward, or backward then forward. One may not trace them forward and then backward under any circumstances. (Asher, 1976, presents the basic theorem of path analysis. This section of our paper assumes familiarity with this basic theorem.) In the case at hand, one can trace the paths between $x_1$ to X to Y and finally to $y_1$ in tracing the path from $x_1$ to $y_1$, and since one goes backward, forward, and forward, this is a legitimate decomposition of the correlation between $x_1$ and $y_1$ into path coefficients.

3. To be statistically accurate, we must distinguish between population parameters and sample estimates (see Appendix A). To be consistent with Appendix A, we should state the equation as:

$$\rho x_1 y_1 = abc$$

where $\rho x_1 y_1$ is the correlation in the population. We then wish to develop estimators for the unknown parameters in terms of the estimable quantity, $\rho x_1 y_1$. Data from a sample is then used to obtain estimates of these parameters using the sample estimate of the correlation, $r_{x_1 y_1}$. To avoid having to introduce new and possibly confusing notation (the multiple-indicator literature generally uses r's rather than $\rho$'s), and having to express everything in terms of both population parameters and sample estimators, we will simplify the presentation somewhat by substituting the sample correlation for the population parameter. We will then "solve" such equations directly for the unknown parameter even though the results are only sample estimates of these paramters based upon the sample estimate of the correlation coefficient. The reader should, however, remain aware of this distinction since it is an important one. The results developed here are sample estimates of population values and, as a result, are subject to the usual sampling problems such as bias and efficiency, *unless* of course the researcher is working with the population of cases rather than a random sample of cases.

4. This hypothesis would be derived from an economic theory of racial discrimination. In the presence of scarce resources, the dominant majority seeks to exclude the racial minority from most major economic activity. In the presence of adequate resources, the most powerful motive (economic self-interest) for discrimination is absent, and although other motives may be present and operative, the result is less economic discrimination than in instances of scarce resources.

5. Campbell and Fiske use the term *trait* in much the same manner that we use the term *abstract concept*. We shall present their method using their term, since it is discussed elsewhere using "trait" rather than "abstract concept" and since it is the multi*trait* matrix.

6. Strictly speaking, the different trait-same method correlations will include more than methodological variance. Although the traits may be conceptually distinct, there will prob-

ably be some causal relationships among them, inflating the correlations above those of pure methodological variance. Generally, one should use the M-M approach with variables which are both conceptually distinct and which have only minor and not powerful direct causal connections among them. If this is true, the common variance between the same concept measured by different methods should still be greater than the common variance between different concepts measured by the same method.

7. All of the models that we present in this paper include only *effect* indicators. The indicators are always conceptualized as effects rather than as causes of the abstract concepts. For a discussion of cause indicators see Namboodiri et al. (1975).

8. All of the multiple-indicator models also contain *conceptual* error terms, labeled $u_i$. These represent all of the unknown causes of the conceptual variables, or constructs. We do not discuss these in the text but include them for the sake of completeness. We assume, of course, that these error terms $u_i$ are uncorrelated with the indicators' error terms, i.e., $E(e_i u_j) = 0$ for all $i = 1, \ldots k$ and $j = 1, \ldots m$ where $k$ = number of indicators and $m$ = number of concepts. We also assume that these conceptual error terms are uncorrelated with each other $E(u_j u_n) = 0$ for all $j, n = 1, \ldots m$. In other words, we assume that all of the unspecified causes of the abstract concepts are random (1) with respect to the errors of measurement in the indicators, (2) with respect to each other, and (3) with respect to the other, specified causes of each concept.

9. As we noted earlier, technically, Equation 8 should be written in terms of the parameters, $\rho$'s, rather than the statistics, $r$'s. Thus sampling error is a problem. See Mayer and Younger (1975) for a test of significance. We discuss this further toward the end of our monograph.

10. The six equations generated by the model in Figure 18 are: (1) $r_{12} = a^2 b$; (2) $r_{13} = a^2 bc$; (3) $r_{14} = a^2 bcd$; (4) $r_{23} = a^2 c$; (5) $r_{24} = a^2 cd$; and (6) $r_{34} = a^2 d$.

11. To see why the estimates of the reliabilities from the model in Figure 19 are unaffected by correlated disturbance terms ($u_i$), consider the following model:

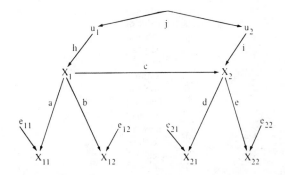

To simplify matters somewhat, let v equal product of paths h, i, and j (this will have no effect on the results derived). The six correlations in the model can be expressed in terms of path coefficients as follows:

$$r_{X_{11}X_{21}} = acd + avd = ad(c + v) \qquad [N-1]$$

$$r_{X_{11}X_{22}} = ace + ave = ae(c + v) \qquad [N-2]$$

$$r_{X_{12}X_{21}} = bcd + bvd = bd(c + v) \qquad [N-3]$$

84

$$r_{X_{12}X_{22}} = bce + bve = be(c + v) \qquad [N\text{-}4]$$

$$r_{X_{11}X_{12}} = ab \qquad [N\text{-}5]$$

$$r_{X_{21}X_{22}} = de. \qquad [N\text{-}6]$$

If one tries to solve for each of the five path coefficients—a, b, c, d, and e—one will note first that no distinct estimate can be derived for c; only c + v can be estimated from these equations. On the other hand, estimates can be easily derived for the four epistemic correlations in the same way this was done for the initial, four-indicator Costner model in Figure 3. If the estimates for these four path coefficients are compared with the estimates that would be derived from the model in Figure 19 (without correlated disturbance terms), they turn out to be exactly the same. The presence of correlated disturbances thus biases the estimate of the true stability, c, but in the calculation of the epistemic correlations v drops out completely and they are thus unbiased. For example, one estimate of d from this model is:

$$d = \sqrt{\frac{r_{X_{11}X_{21}} \cdot r_{X_{21}X_{22}}}{r_{X_{11}X_{22}}}} .$$

## REFERENCES

ALTHAUSER, R. P. and T. A. HEBERLEIN (1970) "Validity and the multitrait-multi-method matrix," pp. 170-184 in E. F. Borgatta and G. W. Bohrnstedt (eds.) Sociological Methodology 1970. San Francisco: Jossey-Bass.
——— and R. A. SCOTT (1971) "A causal assessment of validity: the augmented multitrait-multimethod matrix," pp. 374-399 in H. M. Blalock (ed.) Causal Models in the Social Sciences. Chicago: Aldine.
ASHER, H. (1976) Causal Modeling. Beverly Hills: Sage.
——— (1974) "Some consequences of measurement error in survey data." Amer. J. of Political Sci. 18: 469-485.
BLALOCK, H. M. (1972) Social Statistics. New York: McGraw-Hill.
——— (1970) "Estimating measurement error using multiple indicators and several points in time." Amer. Soc. Rev. 35: 101-111.
——— (1969) "Multiple indicators and the causal approach to measurement error." Amer. J. of Sociology 75: 264-272.
——— (1968) "The measurement problem: a gap between the languages of theory and research," pp. 5-27 in H. M. Blalock and A. B. Blalock (eds.) Methodology in Social Research. New York: McGraw-Hill.
——— (1967) "Causal inferences, closed populations, and measures of association." Amer. Political Sci. Rev. 61: 130-136.
——— (1964) Causal Inferences in Nonexperimental Research. Chapel Hill: Univ. of North Carolina Press.

BOHRNSTEDT, G. W. and T. M. CARTER (1971) "Robustness in regression analysis," pp. 118-146 in H. M. Costner (ed.) Sociological Methodology 1971. San Francisco: Jossey-Bass.

CAMPBELL, D. T. and D. W. FISKE (1959) "Convergent and discriminant validation by the multitrait-multimethod matrix." Psych. Bull. 56: 81-105.

COSTNER, H. L. (1969) "Theory, deduction, and rules of correspondence." Amer. J. of Sociology 75: 245-263.

———— and R. SCHOENBERG (1973) "Diagnosing indicator ills in multiple indicator models," pp. 168-200 in A. S. Goldberger and O. D. Duncan (eds.) Structural Equation Models in the Social Sciences. New York: Seminar.

DAWSON, R. E. and J. A. ROBINSON (1963) "Inter-party competition, economic variables, and welfare policies in the American states." J. of Politics 25: 265-289.

DUNCAN, O. D. (1975a) Introduction to Structural Equation Models. San Francisco: Academic Press.

———— (1975b) "Some linear models for two-wave, two variable panel analysis with one-way causation and measurement error," pp. 285-306 in H. M. Blalock et al. (eds.) Quantitative Sociology: International Perspectives on Mathematical and Statistical Modeling. New York: Academic Press.

DYE, T. R. (1969) "Inequality and civil rights policy in the states." J. of Politics 31: 1080-1097.

EDWARDS, A. L. (1957) The Social Desirability Variable in Personality Assessment and Research. New York: Dryden.

FISHER, F. M. (1966) The Identification Problem in Econometrics. New York: McGraw-Hill.

GUETZKOW, H. and C. H. CHERRYHOLMES (1966) Internation Simulation Kit. Chicago: Science Research Associates.

HANNAN, M. T., R. RUBINSON and J. T. WARREN (1974) "The causal approach to measurement error in panel analysis: some further contingencies," pp. 293-323 in H. M. Blalock (ed.) Measurement in the Social Sciences. Chicago: Aldine.

HAUSER, R. and A. GOLDBERGER (1971) "The treatment of unobservable variables in path analysis," pp. 81-117 in H. Costner (ed.) Sociological Methodology 1971. San Francisco: Jossey-Bass.

HEISE, D. R. (1971) "Separating reliability and stability in test-retest correlation," pp. 348-363 in H. M. Blalock (ed.) Causal Models in the Social Sciences. Chicago: Aldine.

HENKEL, R. E. (1976) Tests of Significance. Beverly Hills: Sage.

JACKSON, D. N., S. A. AHMED and N. A. HEAPY (1976) "Is achievement a unitary construct." J. of Research in Personality 10: 1-21.

JORESKOG, K. G. (1973) "A general method for estimating a linear structural equation system," pp. 85-112 in A. S. Goldberger and O. D. Duncan (eds.) Structural Equation Models in the Social Sciences. New York: Seminar.

———— (1969) "A general approach to confirmatory maximum likelihood factor analysis." Psychometrika 34: 183-202.

———— and D. SORBOM (1977) "Statistical models and methods for analysis of longitudinal data," pp. 285-327 in D. J. Aigner and A. S. Goldberger (eds.) Latent Variables in Socio-Economic Models. Amsterdam: North Holland.

KMENTA, J. (1971) Elements of Econometrics. New York: Macmillan.

LONG, J. S. (1976) "Estimation and hypothesis testing in linear models containing measurement error: a review of Joreskog's model for the analysis of covariance structures." Soc. Methods and Research 5 (November): 157-206.

LORD, F. M. and M. R. NOVICK (1968) Statistical Theories of Mental Test Scores. Reading, MA: Addison-Wesley.

86

MAYER, L. E. and M. S. YOUNGER (1975) "Multiple indicators and the relationship between abstract variables," pp. 191-211 in D. R. Heise (ed.) Sociological Methodology 1975. San Francisco: Jossey-Bass.

NAMBOODIRI, N. K., L. F. CARTER and H. M. BLALOCK (1975) Applied Multivariate Analysis and Experimental Designs. New York: McGraw-Hill.

NUNNALLY, J. C. (1976) Psychometric Theory. New York: McGraw-Hill.

OSGOOD, C. E., G. J. SUCI and P. H. TANNENBAUM (1957) The Measurement of Meaning. Urbana: Univ. of Illinois Press.

RANNEY, A. (1965) "Parties in state politics," p. 65 in H. Jacob and K. N. Vines (eds.) Politics in the American States. Boston: Little, Brown.

SELLTIZ, C., M. JAHODA, M. DEUTSCH and S. W. COOK (1976) Research Methods in Social Relations. New York: Holt, Rinehart & Winston.

SPEARMAN, C. and K. J. HOLZINGER (1924) "The sampling error in the theory of two factors." British J. of Psychology 15: 17-19.

WERTS, C. E., R. L. LINN and K. G. JORESKOG (1971) "Estimating the parameters of path models involving unmeasured variables," pp. 400-413 in H. M. Blalock (ed.) Causal Models in the Social Sciences. Chicago: Aldine.

WHEATON, B., B. MUTHEN, D. ALWIN and G. SUMMERS (1977) "Assessing reliability and stability in panel models," pp. 84-136 in D. Heise (ed.) Sociological Methodology 1977. San Francisco: Jossey-Bass.

WILEY, D. E. and J. A. WILEY (1971) "The estimation of measurement error in panel data," pp. 364-373 in H. M. Blalock (ed.) Causal Models in the Social Sciences. Chicago: Aldine.

*JOHN L. SULLIVAN, Associate Professor of political science at the University of Minnesota, received his undergraduate education at the University of Minnesota and his Ph.D. from the University of North Carolina at Chapel Hill. He is coeditor of* Political Methodology, *a scholarly journal, and has published articles on political behavior and quantitative methods in such journals as* American Political Science Review, American Journal of Political Science, Journal of Politics, *and* International Journal of Political Education. *He is currently involved in research on political tolerance.*

*STANLEY FELDMAN, Assistant Profession of political science at Brown University, received his undergraduate education at the State University of New York at Stony Brook and his Ph.D. from the University of Minnesota. He has published articles on political attitudes and belief systems and on research methodology. He is currently involved in research on cognitive structures in mass belief systems.*

# Quantitative Applications in the Social Sciences

(A Sage University Papers Series)

$3.00 each

SAGE PUBLICATIONS, INC.
P. O. Box 5024
BEVERLY HILLS, CALIF. 90210

PLACE
STAMP
HERE